New Zealand

Literature

Today

In the Same Series

Australian and Indian Literature: Studies in Mutual Response
Ed. David Kerr and R.K. Dhawan

Australian Literature Today
Ed. R.K. Dhawan and David Kerr

New Zealand Literature Today

Edited by
R.K. Dhawan
William Tonetto

Indian Society for Commonwealth Studies

Published by
Indian Society for Commonwealth Studies
New Delhi 110 015.

ISBN 81-85218-69-2

Phototypesetting by
dataculture
New Delhi 110 024

Printed at
Mehra Offset Press
New Delhi 110 002

CONTENTS

Introduction

WALTER TONETTO

> . . . the great thing to learn in this life is to be content with appearances, and to shun the vulgarities of the grocer and philosopher.
>
> Katherine Mansfield

With an awareness for the sesquicentenary of the Treaty of Waitangi, it is an auspicious time to be collecting some views on the strength of New Zealand literature. Allen Curnow's landmark case for a working definition will soon be thirty years old. While treading the piebald patches of his country's literature, Curnow's patrician muse was as doggedly guarded then, as some overvaulting contemporary estimates are flaunting the guide and the compass of the master-surveyor now. Characteristically, Curnow—while acknowledging her to be the equatorial scion that she was—had doubts about including Katherine Mansfield into the fold of New Zealand *literature*. This presents us with a paradox: K.M. and her artefacts are worshipped nationwide in biographies, feature films, critical studies, and are hung in museums and galleries;—the very reason for acceptance of the initials K.M. when referring to her indicates the degree of posthumous affection. Yet from early on she never saw herself as belonging; and indeed, had she remained in New Zealand, it is possible that she may have suffered the fate that has befallen other great women writers: like a sawyer toiling away at his henge in the shade of the pohutukawas, the timber of the self-exiled is invariably cut from the joists of his or her own mind.

Frame, one of the country's finest writers, shows the dangers of self-exile, indicated in the vehemence with which Frame, a copious autobiographer, gives short shrift to her sprightly biographer Patrick Evans, implying a "possessiveness about one's own experience that makes it communicable only by oneself."[1] This "possessiveness" is perhaps nowhere more apparent than in Frame's repeated and obsessive zeal for enumeration in her recent novel *The Carpathians*, a flaw already in her earlier work. Saying this, however, we must remember that Frame's best work (*Faces in the Water, A State of Siege*, and perhaps *The Edge of The Alphabet*) has rightly been compared to Patrick White.

The paradox of K.M. won't go away, since this collection of critical pieces too, while roaming amongst the new and the old in New Zealand literature, has its focus obliquely on her. For whether we like it or not, when talking of greatness in New Zealand writing, the guardian spirit of our confidences (inevitably like the rainbow bows to the earth) first makes his obeisance to the spirit of Mansfield. All things that follow thereafter issue tacitly from this gesture of homage.

While Australia saw its bicentenary out with sulphurous flares stalking the horizon, New Zealand celebrated the centenary of Katherine Mansfield. But as with flares, so with any fanfaronade: the ensuing darkness is more acutely felt, and the sulphur of the final Expo pyrotechnics, mingling with the waters of the Tasman Sea, bring up poignant questions about the Self, and the riddle of cultural belonging. The lodestar, for instance, of Bill Manhire's *The Brain of Katherine Mansfield* brilliantly illustrated by Gregory O'Brien—is a trepanning of that most sacred of reliquaries, K.M.'s brain (with help from Smithyman's "Jelly Beans" thrown in), but also "putting the warts and gumboots on the national portrait," as Iain Sharp with characteristic acerbity observes.[2] But deflating the cultural tyre is not always conducive to swift onward movement, as Manhire discovers when he is hoisted on his own petard in an interview with Hone Tuwhare, the "Elizabethan Maori" (Hulme's phrase). Asking what the future might hold for New Zealand, Tuwhare, tellingly abrasive when the need arises, counsels Manhire to "bloody well get stuffed."[3] Pakeha and Maori sensibilities, Mansfield and the rest, are the inalienable shibboleths of contemporary writing.

Identity and belonging are perhaps not so much negotiated in the usual way, as simply transcended; the writer's spiritual passport, in any case, has always been a *passe-partout*, the lightest kerseymere around the necks of those who, with Oscar Wilde, have very little to declare, which usually later is perceived to be so much; being at home in many nations, he has no home, and the dwelling of permanence he erects is from the start his work, the rotten beams of early efforts and the highly polished floorboards of his final *pied-á-terre*. The house of houses is a papery dome, spiralling beyond brick and mortar to the stratosphere, where uniformity of grace reigns in every direction.

Back in the seventies, Curnow spoke of only a handful of New Zealand writers who mattered, with the number of critics being even smaller, (had he heard of Arno Schmidt's rebarbative calculations?) Perhaps little changes, but there are enough writers of strength today to give meaning to the idea of a national identity—for all the emulative tendency in things of culture—and for a sense of an organic connection to the rest of the world to become possible. While the thirties tapped a rich vein in literature, the late twentieth century in New Zealand has writers at least comparable in stature (and even in number) to the bigger brother across the Tasman Sea. The naevus of callow youthfulness has almost become superseded by a more robust layer of possibilities.

But it is never a question, of course, of numbers, of pitting shredded laurels and awards in some futile reckoning of material excellence. The arts, and the world's artists, may be poor, but their essence remains unassimilable, ever resistant to economic estimate or political quarrel.

This year's International P.E.N. conference in Vienna was convened under the star of mondialism, and it is appropriate to have thus included the American David Ray here, an excellent poet, and wonderful exponent of the *humanitas* that binds all peoples, moving so powerfully into the ascendant. Vincent O'Sullivan, a qasar nourished from the bedrock, perhaps, of Frame's mythopoeic Memory Flower (if you will), is of a different mettle, poetically, and reading their work side-by-side here is for a moment to note the differing trajectories of this poetic game of battledore and shuttlecock. For poetry, in the beginning and in the end, is a thing of unremitting joy, and thus a thing to be frolicked with, piercing in its finest moments effortlessly the pavise of our guardedness; moments when silence becomes one vibration, and attentiveness swiftly delivers gifts of direct knowing.

Thus the Steads, Braschs, Manhires and O'Sullivans: through them New Zealand lives, but it lives in many more names, some of which haven't even made it into the representative and carefully selected anthologies. Too much cogitation spells disaster in verse, and yet the disastrous estimate (of those who do not write) continues—as elsewhere in the world—to determine what is worthy and what is feathers, yet flying not by direction of the grounded theoreticians. Not that anthologers are all stupid people, but theory increasingly determines a creature's airworthiness, even though it be of an aquatic disposition. But life goes on in the margins, around the robust spines of books, keeping those who make it between the covers honest, providing the leaven in a cultural awakening of which everyone is a part.

A few words about drama. Let us take a glance at the International Festival of the Arts in Wellington at the beginning of 1988. Neil Gudsell's cabaret sketches, which formed part of the program, "expressed the aching sadness of the lost soul," the malaise of post industrialist societies everywhere[4]; but it was even more important for the enunciation to Pakeha sensibility of the five principles of Maori theatre, the most important of which are: *Mahi* (work undertaken from communal love), *Manuhinitanga* (hospitality to guest and stranger) and *Korero* (speech that begets peace and understanding). Harbouring pent-up frustrations, and perhaps no aid to the cause of non-violence, was the performance of Julianne O'Brien's *The Rainbow Warrior*, capturing the events surrounding the sinking of the Greenpeace Warrior, and the release of the French assassins in violation of a U.N. Agreement. In 1991, of course, the French Government had the chutzpah to award one of its highest military honours to one former agent, a terrorist of the State. May the pens be dipped once more in vitriol, and indite such unfathomable and provocative stupidity!

The New Zealander, a play by Joseph Mesaglin, showed the siege at the office of Samuel Quick, editor of "The New Zealander" in Auckland in 1864, in the aftermath of the Battle of Gate Pa; while Maoris accuse Quick of highlighting the navy's cowardice and thereby undervaluing their heroism. Her Majesty's navy is aggrieved at Quick's reportage of their debacle. In a splendid dream sequence, Quick is visited by a glistening near-naked warrior and an urbane gentleman, and all sit together, taking tea. When we survey New Zealand drama, we have to aver from the outset that, as with Broadway (and unlike Australia), New Zealand tabloids favour overnight reviewing; indeed, when the reviewing is good, it facilitates true reciprocity between drama and audience, as well as helps underscore the living character of the play. While novels or poetry tend towards a more open assemblage of purpose and gift, plays often narrow that focus; great movements in drama as a whole might for that reason become discernible only over a longer period. In drama, the nation lives most acutely, since (as Yeats had said) "we only believe those thoughts which have been conceived not in the brain but in the whole body." Poetic drama would thus be the most nourishing of life's forms, conceived in the soul and the body, and bodied forth once more on stage. On this score, alas, the nation still lags behind the finest achievement evident elsewhere.

The Pacific crown, if such thing existed in our post-colonial times, would undoubtedly have to be wrested from the Faustian skull that one imagines Manhire to have placed on his desk at Victoria University. The hand committing such heartening larceny would be none other than Sione Falesi's, obstinate octogenarian, and grand purveyor of humour in Dr Edell Hau'ofa's *Tales of the Tikongs* (first published in 1983); Hau'ofa's *Kisses in the Nederends*, published five years ago, followed its predecessor, remarkable again for the intelligence of its humour, and the ribaldry of its theme. *Tales* is a delightful decameron, and perhaps the only book, excepting Nancy Phelan's *Serpents in Paradise*, that is genuinely humorous: "rare wit and entertainment . . . from a writer previously unknown bring burst of unexpected pleasure."[5] But the yield in trout and salmon may well be richer in these waters: there is little serious-eyed writing in the Pacific, and probably less need for the soul-searching of big and often misbegotten nations.

NOTES

1. Evans, *Untold*, 6, Spring 1986, p. 2.
2. *Landfall*, 167, September 1988, p. 328.
3. Ibid., p. 278.
4. Cooke, *Dominion Sunday Times*, 3 April 1988, p. 11.
5. McLauchlan, *Auckland Star*, June 1983, p. 34.

New Zealand Literature Today

R.K. DHAWAN

I

New Zealand literature is perhaps the youngest literature in the white Commonwealth and, amongst the new literatures, a significant one. It has been increasingly realized that this literature is as rich and varied as other literatures written elsewhere, say in England, America, or Australia. In recent years, writers such as Frank Sargeson, Janet Frame, Dan Davin, James Baxter, Maurice Duggan, Maurice Gee, C.K. Stead, Patricia Grace, Keri Hulme and Vincent O'Sullivan have contributed significantly to the substance and quality of New Zealand writing. Now that New Zealand has established a rich literary tradition of its own, with several poets and novelists articulating a genuine voice of a distinct culture, one is tempted to make a systematic evaluation of the literary contribution made by the contemporary writers. It was my visit to the University of Western Australia, Perth, in November 1991 that made this special volume on New Zealand literature possible. The three scholars whom I met there and who inspired me in this area were: Vincent O'Sullivan, eminent New Zealand poet; David Ray, American Professor who has written some remarkable poems on New Zealand; and Suzette Henke who is a specialist on Keri Hulme. Walter Tonetto, my co-editor, extended all his help and cooperation in the preparation of this volume. My gratitude to all of them.

II

New Zealand, for long uninhabited, was discovered in comparatively recent times by Polynesians. Originally from South-east Asia, the Polynesian peoples had progressively spread across the Pacific and eventually reached Aotearon, or New Zealand. Those who settled here have come to be known as Maoris. The study of Maori society before AD 1769 is largely the study of the adaptation of a group of Polynesians to this new land in which they found themselves. The people during that time lived by hunting, fishing, gardening, and the gathering of plant foods. Situation changed in the last decade of the 18th century, with the advent of the explorers and traders. And finally the more permanent settlers started arriving in the late 1830s. These groups added to the variety of social developments as they differed distinctly both in their purpose and nature. As the British settlers spread over the country, their search for land brought them into contact with the Maoris, with the result that a series of campaigns were fought in the eighteen sixties. Having overpowered the Maoris, the British settlers had easy access to the land which they sought and the immigration from England increased substantially.

Since the early colonists were predominantly the Britishers, the nineteenth century New Zealand's economy was dependent on the United Kingdom. New Zealand provided mainly food and fruit products of value to British importers but in technology and industry, she banked totally on Britain. Apart from this economic relationship, there developed relationship with the eastern Australian colonies, from which a pastoral economy was derived. In the early colonial years New Zealand traded through Australian ports and to a great extent reflected Australian business trends. This trading relationship later declined, especially when Australia started emerging as strong competitor rather than a mere neighbouring trading centre.

III

The origin of literature in New Zealand was essentially English. It is indeed difficult to segregate some of the early New Zealand writings from those of English or even Australian. In order to give an identity, the writers felt it necessary to record specifically New Zealand experience which is evident in the writings of Jessie Mackay, Blanche Baughan and William Satchell in the early decades of the twentieth century. Most of the writers showed a concern with history, landscape, society and human relationship. This generalized sense of the "New Zealandness" became evident in most of the writings in the early decades of the present century.

Curiously, literary critical debate in New Zealand has focused on poetry or short story rather than novel or drama. The main reason for this is that poetry is easily gathered into anthologies which find a good response with the under-populated country. No wonder, the publication of poetry or a short-story anthology, with a significant editorial introduction, in this country has always been a major cultural event, a literary celebration.

James Baxter (1926-72), internationally known, was the son of a writer. He believed in poetry as a "cell of good living in a corrupt society." Apart from poetry, he wrote a number of plays which were well received. Keith Sinclair (b. 1922) is essentially an academic historian by profession. He has written an excellent history of New Zealand. He began writing taking Donne as his model but later turned to Yeats, and Graves. His poetry reveals his profound knowledge of the Maoris. C.K. Stead (b. 1932) is a renowned lucid and thoughtful critic. Besides being a critic, he has written a sufficient number of poems and a political novel, *Smith's Dream* (1971). In this novel, Stead asks us to imagine ourselves living under a different kind of government.

IV

The main tradition of short-story writing is a highly sophisticated one, involving narrative indirection and a commitment to open and broken forms. The main bearers of this tradition in New Zealand writing are Katherine Mansfield, Frank Sargeson and Maurice Duggan, and among contemporary writers Vincent O'Sullivan, Witi Ihimaera and Patricia Grace.

Katherine Mansfield is perhaps the first significant New Zealand writer. She was educated in London, and settled down in Europe at the age of twenty. She married the eminent English critic John Middleton Murry in 1918 and escaped provincialism. She had an instinct for writing and attained utmost popularity as a short-story writer. She is an autobiographical writer and her best stories are the ones which depict her childhood in New Zealand.

Katherine Mansfield was an adept teller of tales, and has rightly been called a writer's writer. Mansfield's international reputation as one of the world's best-known short-story writers is based on a collection of eighty-eight stories. As raw material of her fiction, she chose ordinary, commonplace incidents. And her characters were not heroic persons; she portrayed the average human beings with their feelings and emotions.

There is a continuing interest in her life and work. A contributory factor to the growth of her popularity was the act of Middleton Murry in publishing her carefully edited letters and journals. Some of her stories like "Prelude," "The Daughters of the Late Colonel" and "At the Bay" are similar to novels in that they are divided into twelve sections or episodes. Her technical innovations and skill as evident in these stories have made a significant influence on modern writing.

When Mansfield died on January 9, 1923 at the age of thirty-four, she had published three books of short-stories. In addition to her fiction, Mansfield left a body of writing of another kind. She was a prolific correspondent, a good writer of diaries and notebooks and a busy reviewer. In her will she bequeathed all 'manuscripts and letters' to her husband but she cautioned: "I should like him to publish as little as possible and tear up" the rest. Murry however took care not to destroy anything and, during the course of time, published all that he had with him.

Apart from Katherine Mansfield, other women writers who have achieved some measure of literary fame outside their country are— Sylvia Ashton-Warner and Janet Frame. There is something common in the three writers: the fictions of all of them are forms of autobiography while autobiography borders on fiction.

V

Novel developed slowly in New Zealand when compared to short story or poetry. Indeed there was scant production in the mid-decades of the century. Main reason for this has been the paucity of publishing avenues. Bringing out a novel has been too expensive a venture for small presses to embark on. It would simply be not a viable proposition financially. Of the New Zealand publishers only the commercial firm of A.H. and A.W. Reed brought out more than two novels during the thirties and forties. Between 1940 and 1951, for example, the country produced thirteen novels and six short-story collections, Three authors Frank Sargeson, Roderick Finlayson and Dan Davin alone wrote nine of these volumes. The local market had been much too small compared with that of a British publisher who had the support of colonial sales as well as those in the homeland. No wonder, the creative writers looked first to the English publisher. This difficulty of getting novels published in their country induced New Zealand writers to favour the short-story.

During and after the Second World War, the New Zealanders faced the problem of identity. There was depression, recovery and surge of hope it brought. The country, during mid-decades, passed through an intense time, and witnessed a colonial society transformed into an independent one. This led to the renaissance, the birth of awakening in literature and art. A host of writers, including Katherine Mansfield, John A. Lee and Robin Hyde successfully attempted in establishing a descernible New Zealand literature identity in literature.

John Alexander Lee (b. 1891) became a Labour M.P. between the two world wars and was expelled by his party in 1940. He was in parliament when his first novel, *Children of the Poor*, was published. It is an autobiographical novel and offended many because it told the truth. In it, Lee told the story of his slum boyhood and of his sister's prostitution. His succeeding novels tell the story of war and of Lee's delinquent boyhood over again. Sylvia Ashton-Warner (1908-84) was a teacher. Her novel *Spinster* (1958) has gained the status of a minor classic. It is the tale of the school year of a gifted teacher, Anna Vorontosov, who in many ways is like its creator. In *Bell Call* (1965), the story is narrated by a ghost and her mortal husband. Maurice Duggan (1922-1975) was a fastidious writer, modest and with a small output (two books of stories, a novella, and a couple of books of children's stories), but his achievement was considerable.

Frank Sargeson (b. 1903) has been the most influential and celebrated novelist New Zealand has produced. Like many New Zealand writers, Sargeson began as a satirist and his first pamphlet of stories *Conversation with My Uncle* (1936) satirized suburban life. Subsequently however he has gone on to make emancipation and spiritual redemption his main theme. For a number of years, he wrote stories only. He achieved popularity with the publication of *That Summer* (1943). Once his genius flourished he wrote a number of novels. *Sunset Village* (1979), set in present-day Auckland, is a story of a group of old-age pensioners. It is a good comical novel. In fact, the best introduction to Sargeson's novels is to be found in the three novels collected in *Man of England Now*. The title story follows the life of an English immigrant through a long working life in New

Zealand.

Maurice Gee is one of the major New Zealand writers. He has written adult fiction, children's fiction, and television scripts. His novel *Plumb* (1978) won him the New Zealand Fiction Award, and *Meg* (1983) won the New Zealand Award for Fiction. His significant publications include *The Big Season* and *Sole Survivor*.

Dan Davin (b. 1913) grew up in Invercargill, and was educated at Catholic schools, Otago University, and Balliol College, Oxford. He worked as academic publisher to the University Press in Oxford, London, for more than thirty years. His short stories are collected in *The Gorse Blooms Pale* (1947). These are set in an area of South Canterbury settled by Irish Catholics, and in the Middle East during the Second World War. There are eight stories about childhood, seven about students or the life of transients in New Zealand and London, and eleven stories about war. Davin's first novel *Cliffs of Fall* (1945) focuses on the aberrations of a man of exceptional talent who sets himself above the law. *For the Rest of Our Lives* (1947) is considered Davin's best novel. Based on his war experiences, the novel of seventy-six short chapters gives us a New Zealander at war. *Roads from Home* (1949) is set in New Zealand, *The Sullen Bell* (1956) in London. *Not Here, Not Now* (1970) concludes the sequence of New Zealand novels. It is a painfully detailed re-creation and documentation of those Depression years that threw a shadow of economic hardship and radical politics across the normally carefree life of students at Otago University. *Brides of Price* (1972) is light-hearted in its approach. *The Selected Stories* (1981) contains the distillation of Davin's genius in this form. Many of the stories are of childhood, unobtrusive and cxtremely sensitive.

Janet Frame (b. 1924) is a writer who has gained an international reputation. She began with a promising trilogy: *Owls Do Cry* (1957), *Faces in the Water* (1961) and *The Edge of the Alphabet* (1962). In fact, since the publication of *Owls Do Cry*, some thirty-five years ago, Frame has established herself as a significant modern novelist. This novel of hers was reissued in 1961 by the Women's Press, whose cover makes a case for abandoning the colonial qualifier and acknowledging her "as one of the most considerable novelists worldwide." When the novel was released, it was supposed to be a landmark, an innovative literary work. To the readers, it was a difficult first novel. Unlike other contemporary novels, it is not written in simple English prose. Nor does it tell a story as a series of clearly described events. The novelist does not ever stand back and let us know what is happening. The experiences she describes are very special, very private ones. She tries to show the inner lives of intense, often unhappy, people. The novel is a tale of metamorphosis, of one Daphene's transformation. In Depression New Zealand the Withers family—Toby, Nicks, Daphene and their parents—live out their blighted lives. The children play amid the refuse of the rubbish dump that seems the perfect metaphor for the marginal existence. But there is treasure as well, old books and ledgers. The novelist portrays peculiar people, in a peculiar way. She tries to show us just how such people think, and how they experience the world. In a way, she tells us that traditional ways of writing novels are not suited to the kinds of people and experiences she aims to describe.

On the other hand, Frame in *Owls Do Cry* adopts a new method. She tries to take us inside the feelings, minds, and experiences of her charracters. And that is why the novel has affinities with such books as *A Portrait of the Artist as a Young Man*, *Ulysses*, *The Sound and the Fury*, and *To the Lighthouse*. Frame continues to establish the tradition of psychological novel, started by Joseph Conrad and D.H. Lawrence, and perfected by Virginia Woolf and Dorothy Richardson.

VI

The Maoris are said to have travelled from Asia to Tahiti and its neighbouring islands. They carried with them a mythology that matched with their own great qualities. These myths and legends have been a subject of great research. As early as the mid-nineteenth century, Sir George Grey's *Polynesian Mythology* was published—a book that made a mark in academic world. In the recent years, a reliable and useful study of this subject is available in the book entitled *Maori Myths and Tribal Legends* as narrated by Anthony Alpers. This book is divided into two parts. The first part contains mythology proper of the Maori. These are the myths these people brought to New Zealand from "Hawaiki." For example, they have a Creation myth of surpassing beauty, a pantheon of gods and heroes worthy to rival those of the Greeks. Part Two gives a selection of the best stories, related to their descent from the gods and demi-gods we learn of in Part I.

We must note that Maoris have a long tradition of poetry. The manuscripts of the early collections of Maori poetry are kept in public libraries in New Zealand. Two eminent scholars, Apirana Nagata and Pei Te Hurinui arranged a monumental collection of three hundred poems, giving the historical significance and linguistic analysis of these.

Witi Ihimaera and Patricia Grace are two distinguished Maori writers of fiction. Compared to the traditional Maori writers, they are less didactic and better acquainted with the range of English literature. Witi Ihimaera is the award-winning author of *Pounamu Pounamu*, *Tangi*, *Whanau* and *Maori*. Born in 1944, he is of Maori descent. A career diplomat with the New Zealand Ministry of Foreign Affairs, Ihimaera is a renowned commentator on Maori and Pacific issues. He has been New Zealand Counsul, New York. Until the publication of Witi Ihimaera's *Tangi* (1973), the first novel by a Maori writer, Maori writing in English had mainly been confined to the journal *Te Ao Hau*. Ihimaeras's novel was an important event and a challenge to a readership accustomed to European New Zealand literary and cultural traditions. *Tangi* mixes traditional oral features of Maori culture with the conventions of the novel form. A large number of Ihimaera's stories are told in third person, sometimes from the point of view of a male character; sometimes from that of an observer. Like Joseph Conrad, he aimed at providing as many viewpoints as he could so that the reader would make his own judgements.

Patricia Grace has been publishing short-stories and novels since the mid-1970s and, like Ihimaera, she dramatizes a strongly Maori way of seeing and experiencing the world. Memory plays an important part in her stories, not only because it enables one to connect a lost past with a turbulent present, but because it is a significant part of Maori folk tradition. The predominant mode of her stories is first-person narration, usually from the point of view of the central character. She creates a prose style based on the structure of Maori speech and evokes the rhythm of the speech of the old people she had heard tell stories. In terms of style, she partakes many qualities of the stylists such as Virginia Woolf, Patrick White, Katherine Mansfield, Frank Sargeson and Janet Frame.

Keri Hulme (b. 1947), a major contemporary writer, started her career as a tobacco picker. She also served as a fish and chop cook. Subsequently, she became T.V. director. She studied law before becoming full-time writer. The most spectacular literary event in New Zealand in the last decade was the publication of Keri Hulme's *The Bone People*. Rejected by several established publishers, it was brought out by a women's collective, *Spiral*, was a huge success in New Zealand and went on to win the Booker Prize in Britain in 1985. This success has also produced a critical reaction. C.K. Stead has raised the question of the author's racial identity and has argued there is something spurious and opportunistic in its Maoriness. There has also been a wider cultural backlash against the novel's sympathetic identification with Maoritanga. Its title has become a term of abuse for Pakeha "fellow-travellers." Hulme's novel has become a political event rather than a mere literary text.

Hulme is of mixed Pakeha and Maori ancestry and she addresses both a Maori and Pakeha readership. In *The Bone People*, the central male character is mainly Maori but part-European. The leading female character is mainly European but part-Maori, and the child, Simon/Haimona, also is the son of ship-wrecked European parents. The novel uses this configuration of hybridity to explore tensions in New Zealand's mixed culture in a more complex manner than these generalizations about its ideological role allow.

The Bone People accepts that New Zealand, the largest Polynesian country in the world, is inescapably multi-cultural, and explores many implications of this. It does not accept that only Maoris can speak about Maoritanga, nor does it accept that Pakeha representations of multi-culturalness are bound to be either oppressive or romanticized. As someone of English, Maori and Orkney-Scots descent, Hulme writes out of the heart of New Zealand's contemporary condition.

VII

The present volume contains some significant poems, which are representative samples of the kind of poetry being written in New Zealand now. We have chosen poets whose work is distinctive, varied and likely to appeal to readers. A remarkable quality of the new poetry is the change from the traditional 'closed' form of English writing to an 'open' form. Several New Zealand poets have come to realize that poetry need not necessarily have a beginning, a middle and an end. The emphasis in the writing tends to move away from the traditional 'content.'

A mention may be made about some of the poets whose poems are included here. Vincent O'Sullivan needs no introduction; he is one of the established literary figures of New Zealand. Marshall Walker is an academic; we look forward to more poems from him. Again, Riemke Ensing is an academic from the University of Auckland. David Ray, an American Professor, has written some excellent poems on New Zealand. Jan Kemp has been an expatriate New Zealand writer for the past ten years. She has undertaken various assignments and has taught at the University of Hongkong and East Asia at Macau. Currently, she is a lecturer in the English Language Proficiency Unit at the National University of Singapore. She has published substantially, and her latest anthology of poems entitled *The Other Hemisphere* uses images from Europe, Asia and the Pacific.

VIII

New Zealand has to face a double challenge—from the mother-country England as also from her immediate neighbour, Australia. Indeed she does not have a Shakespeare nor a Patrick White, but she does have some significant writers—like Frank Sargeson and Janet Frame, not to talk of Katherine Mansfield—who have been accorded international recognition and are rated amongst the best.

The present selection of critical essays and creative writing is designed to represent various directions in which literary trends have been taking shape in New Zealand over the last few years, and to suggest possible developments in the near future. The anthology, it is hoped, amply reflects the wealth and variety of innovative and inventive writing being practised and published in New Zealand.

Select Bibliography

Alpers, Antony, Retold by. *Maori and Tribal Legends*. New Zealand: Longman Paul, 1986.

Cox, H.M.L., ed. *Ten Modern New Zealand Poets*. Auckland: Longman Paul, 1982.

Coyle, Martin, *et al*, ed. *Encyclopedia of Literature and Criticism*. London: Routledge, 1991.

Davin, D.M., ed. *New Zealand Short Stories*. New Zealand: Oxford University Press, 1976.

Hankin, Cherry, ed. *Critical Essays on the New Zealand Short Story*. Auckland: Heinemann, 1982.

Oliver, W.H., ed. *The Oxford History of New Zealand*. Wellington: Oxford University press, 1981.

O'Sullivan, Vincent, Selected by. *An Anthology of Twentieth Century New Zealand Poetry*. London: Oxford University Press, 1976.

Paterson, Alistair, ed. *Contemporary New Zealand Poets*. New Zealand: Pilgrims South Press, 1980.

Seymour-Smith, Martin. *Macmillan Guide to Modern World Literature*. Macmillan Reference Books, 1985.

Sinclair, Keith. *A History of New Zealand*. Auckland: Penguin Books, 1980.

Stead, C.K. *In the Glass Case: Essays on New Zealand Literature*. Auckland: Auckland University Press, 1981.

Wedd, Ian, and Harvey McQueen, ed. *The Penguin Book of New Zealand Verse*. Auckland: Penguin Books, 1987.

Wevers, Lydia, ed. *New Zealand Short Stories*. Auckland: Oxford University Press, 1986.

Katherine Mansfield: A Rare Writer with a Unique Vision and Voice

K. VENKATA REDDY

Perhaps the first New Zealand writer to be accepted and naturalized in the domain of English letters was Katherine Mansfield. She was also certainly the first among that little band of English writers who staked their whole future on the short story which had mainly been the occasional by-product of a novelist. And it stands to the unquestionable credit of Katherine Mansfield that she could give the English short story not only a new content but also a new form. She brought to the short story the sensibility of a poet and breathed into it the life spirit of poetry. Like Henry James, Proust, Joyce, Dorothy Richardson and Virginia Woolf, Katherine Mansfield extended the range of fiction by developing new methods of capturing and conveying the atmosphere of the mind and translating the subtle nuances of human thought and feeling into words.

Katherine Mansfield's literary bent manifested itself at the age of nine when she could get a short story published in a magazine called *The Lone Hand*. Soon after the completion of her school education, she was sent to Queen's College, London. During her first years in London, her interests turned to music and she aspired to be a musician.

But, much against her will, she had to return in 1906 to her native town, Wellington, where she passed the next two years, rebelling against the narrowness of a remote provincial existence. However, she succeeded in her attempt to persuade her father to allow her to go back to London in 1909.

Now, she turned her attention from music to literature and started writing stories. But her stories, which made a complete break from the English short story tradition, were rejected by one publisher after another. She found it difficult to make both ends meet. In her state of depression, she entered into an unhappy marriage with George Bowden whom she left the very next day. Her misery and wretchedness were reflected in the first part of her 1911 volume, *In a German Pension*.

In was in December 1911 that Katherine Mansfield met Middleton Murry who had a profound influence on her life. They lived together as man and wife for six years from 1912 to 1918 when they married. She left England for Bandol in the South of France where she completed her first major work, *The Aloe*, a long story of her childhood days, which set the pattern for all her later work.

Always delicate in health, Katherine Mansfield became increasingly oppressed by illness, and the rest of her life was a constant battle against consumption. All the same, she planned and produced 88 stories (fifteen of which were unfinished) which finally established her as "the most remarkable short story writer of her generation in England." Her last year was spent mostly in Paris. She retired to Fontainblean in October 1922 and died there suddenly on January 9, 1923 at the age of 34, invariably reminding us of the immature death of the immortal poetic artists like Keats and Shelley.

Katherine Mansfield's reputation as a short story writer rests on five volumes of stories--*In a German Pension* (1911), her early work, *Bliss and Other Stories* (1920), *The Garden Party and Other Stories* (1922), *The Dove's Nest and Other Stories* (1923) and *Something Childish* (1924). They were not easily written, but very carefully, even anxiously brooded over in her mind and, what is more, subjected to severe self-criticism in the writing.

In a German Pension is a series of sketches based on Katherine Mansfield's experiences in Germany. These stories, often sharply and crisply satirical, portray many of the Germans as a gross people preoccupied with mountains of food and long detailed discussions of their digestive processes, but covering their grossness and vulgarity with a thick coating of sentimental allegiance to the spirit of the soul. The stories demonstrate this combination of vulgarity and sentimentality with acid sharpness. Although these stories are sensitive and moving portraits of people and their society, they show that Mansfield had not yet found her own style. Crisply and economically told, they are not always completely realized in their effects, however, and often without that sharply focused point of view that she later developed.

Katherine Mansfield's talent as a short story writer had genuinely developed by the time she published the volume, *Bliss and Other Stories*. Her range of subjects had become wider: marriage, people alone in London and trying to make their way in a difficult world, family relationships and little ironic episodes. What is more, Katherine Mansfield's technique had become much surer and more effective. In these stories the writer probes the truths of experience on several different levels of life not limited by social class or interest in the arts or the life of leisure.

Katherine Mansfield's next volume, *The Garden Party and Other Stories*, contains a number of her best-known works-- "The Garden Party" and "Her First Ball" which recapture a great deal of a young girl's experience on entering the social world. In "Her First Ball," Miss Mansfield shows that in the midst of wonder and pleasure comes an awareness of age and the realization that no human experience lasts. Yet the feeling of excitement is genuine and beautifully conveyed. The writer is at her best. She is able to use her style and her crisp language as part of what she wants to say.

In several of the unfinished stories published in *The Dove's Nest and Other Stories*, Katherine Mansfield uses the technique of the stream-of-consciousness as a means to probe more deeply into issues involved in the experiences of her characters. Yet, she retains the ability to use the small, telling detail, the casual conversation, or the intimate mannerism, as a way of displaying more profound and important truths.

Though Katherine Mansfield has a deep concern for virtuous life and moral honesty, the total body of Katherine Mansfield's work does not place her on the side of Victorian virtue. In several stories she satirizes the domestic tyrant who, representing old-fashioned virtues, preys on his daughters. She ridicules the successful and virtuous prude who has neither time nor insight to observe what is going on around him. The people she castigates are, like those *In a German Pension*, the brutal, the callous, the pretentious, the falsely sentimental and the unconcerned. In other words, Katherine Mansfield's stories attempt to describe the truth of the human experience and to praise honesty, directness and fidelity without being tendentious.

Katherine Mansfield is a rare short story writer with a unique vision and voice. Her vision of life expresses itself in the three principal themes--children, men and women, and woman alone--which she treats in a manner that is quite characteristic of her. Her voice is heard in the total articulation of her themes through the techniques--point of view, interior monologue, symbol and lyric language which she employs most creatively and originally.

Katherine Mansfield is known for her unique portrayal of children in her stories. Slipping, as she does, back into the state of childhood, she portrays children as children, showing them as seen through their own eyes and the eyes of other children. Unlike most other writers, she makes a creative use of children to present the adults.

Katherine Mansfield's stories are interesting for the exquisite depiction of the relationship between man and woman as lovers and as husband and wife. If some stories show men and women for whom a happy relation seems impossible because of a predatory or indifferent male, in some other stories the situation is reversed. A happy married relationship is apparent only in the stories which are based on her own parents.

Yet another distinguishing feature of Mansfield's stories is her superb presentation of the woman alone in society, as Mansfield had been in her own life. If her early stories present young women dreaming of bright and happy married life despite their sordid loneliness, the later stories present relatively older women with a growing sense of defeat in their lives.

Though most of her earlier stories rely upon the first-person narration and the dramatic mode, Katherine Mansfield gains a greater dexterity in her narrative technique with the advance of years. As a result, the authorial voice in most of her mature stories is either mute or subdued and the reader is placed directly within the consciousness of the character.

Katherine Mansfield makes a conscious use of the interior monologue as a literary device to give a realistic inside view of her characters. She differs from her contemporaries like Joyce, Virginia Woolf and Dorothy Richardson in her creative use of the interior monologue. Taken directly from the psychological sketch, her "interior monologue" is indirect, stylized, filtered through third person and syntactically conventional narration.

Katherine Mansfield makes use of symbols to communicate the essence of a character or situation, and to create a mood or evoke a theme which is not directly stated. In a Mansfield story almost every detail has a symbolic as well as a narrative function. The symbols add a new dimension to her stories and intensify their effect by extending their depth as well as breadth.

Katherine Mansfield's lyric use of language is praiseworthy. Her sensitive prose with its rhythmical movement, rich imagery and carefully controlled tone and inflexions, is a fit vehicle for the throb of emotion infused into her stories. A close study of her language reveals that almost every character of her mature stories, irrespective of age, sex or station in life, talks in its own special language individual to it with its own voice and its own particular intonation.

The short stories of Katherine Mansfield have received considerable critical attention. If some critics like Conrad Aiken extolled her stories, some others like Frank O'Connor denounced them altogether. The critical studies of her stories by Berkmen and Alpers are, of course, balanced, but they are more biographical than critical. Critics like Ian A. Gordon, Elizabeth Bowen and William Walsh do make a sensible approach to some of her stories, but the scope of their works is too narrow to cover the gamut of Katherine Mansfield's fictional art.

Katherine Mansfield is, par excellence, a fictional artist. The object of her art is not to propose or impose anything, but to explore the core of life, the inner realities, thereby bringing out the unplumbed depths of human experience. Her aim is not to exhibit any technical feat, but to stress the uniqueness of the human personality and to show life as a series of emotional intensities. To achieve this aim, she slips into the minds of her characters and reveals them from inside. She seldom outlines and never dissects a character. What she does is to cause the person to expose himself. The living and breathing reality of her characters astonishes us. They belong to life.

The art of Katherine Mansfield's short story is, by its very nature, tentative, responsive and exploratory. She has no fixed concept of the short story. She goes on experimenting upto the end of her career. There are no signs of casting about to find a formula. Her sense of the possibilities of the story is bounded by no hard-and-fast horizons. Ever on the move, she has left with us no "typical" Katherine Mansfield story to anatomize.

The stories of Katherine Mansfield are moments, instants and gleams of life to which she has given touches of eternity. In her verve, raciness, husky, sensuous poetry, life-likeness and, above all, in her sense of moment's drama, she is almost unrivalled in the history of the English short story. Her masterpieces like "Prelude," "Bliss" and "The Garden Party" have an air of serene inevitability, almost a touch of the miraculous.

Set in New Zealand, "Prelude" centers around a family called "Burnell," a set of characters she also used in a number of later stories which, like "Prelude," are undoubtedly autobiographical to some extent. The Burnell family consists of three young daughters (one of them, Kezia, withdrawn and sensitive, one prissy and domineering, one slow and clumsy), their sensitive mother who hated bearing children, their energetic and successful father, their competent grandmother, and their pretty maiden aunt who is lonely and waiting for a man who never comes. "Prelude" is a series of scenes showing the interactions of these characters on one another against a domestic background. The scenes are given in turn from the point of view of Kezia, the mother, and Beryl, the lonely spinster aunt. The work is full of perceptive passages, sensitive descriptions of nature and of flowers, and a warm understanding of people.

"Bliss" is an effective tale of a modern woman, sensitive and withdrawn, married to a vital and energetic man. The woman finds herself attracted, as she has never been to her husband, to a mysterious and enigmatic Miss Fulton. While giving a dinner party, with Miss Fulton present, the woman suddenly realizes that this attraction, this happiness she feels is really sexual and really directed toward her husband. She is anxious for her guests to leave so that she may begin a new and deeper relationship with him. As the guests are leaving, she accidentally catches a glimpse of her husband in a situation of familiarity with Miss Fulton and the young wife's new-found happiness is shattered.

"The Garden Party" is a single character's story in almost a straightforward sequential narrative. It is occupied with the events of a day in the rich colonial family of Sheridans in New Zealand. As in Jane Austen's novels, the central figure of the story, Laura, is the consciousness through which everything is observed throughout the day's events. The whole story is focused on Laura, a young girl of growing individuality, and her adolescent encounter with death. It seeks to unravel the coexistence of incongruities in life.

Katherine Mansfield was not a rebel, but essentially an innovator. She neither revolted against her predecessors nor broke with them. She simply passed beyond them. She worked by herself in her field. Throughout, she had no guide but her own light. Chekhov was her ally, but not her authority, as her own husband, Murry, made it clear. In both theme and technique, Katherine Mansfield has had an enormous influence on a generation of writers attempting to see things clearly and artistically express them with fidelity and insight. She has shown to her successors in English short story how to control material and insight for disciplined artistic effect. Thus, as a meticulous craftman and a writer committed to a deep sense of moral honesty, Katherine Mansfield is, indeed, a rare creative artist with a unique vision and voice.

Katherine Mansfield: A Study

S. RAMASWAMY

> I believe that people are like portmanteaux--packed with certain things, started going, thrown about, tossed away, dumped down, lost and found, half emptied suddenly, or squeezed fatter than ever, until finally the Ultimate Porter swings them on to the Ultimate Train and away they rattle.[1]
>
> Katherine Mansfield

I

Christopher Isherwood the novelist has said:

> I realize that I loved Mansfield ("Kathy" sounds mawkish now, and "Miss Mansfield" absurdly formal) for her life rather than for her work. I identified myself romantically with her sufferings and her struggle. And today I still find it imposible to think of Mansfield simply as the author of her stories without relating her to the Journal and the Letters. For she is among the most personal and subjective of all modern writers; and in her case, fiction and autobiography form a single indivisible opus.[2]

The critics Clare Hanson and Andrew Gurr are of the same opinion:

> Her life and her fiction were tightly interlocked. She became, in fact, better known as a personality than as a writer, a perspective which is still with us today.[3]

Taking a cue from these two statements, the present writer would like to make a brief study of Katherine Mansfield, taking into account not only her short stories but also her *Journal*,[4] *Letters*[5] and her *Critical Writings*[6] with a special reference to Tradition and Modernity.

The awareness of Tradition and the emergence into Modernity, the demands of New Zealand on the one hand and the Continent--especially England, France and Germany–on the other for representation in her stories, the themes of alienation and internationalism, roots and cosmopolitanism, belonging and exilement, her native and expatriate sensibility, the struggle between Innocence and Experience, and more than anything else, her zest for life--joi de vivre--and her tuberculosis which had condemned her for an early death with the resulting agony and suffering--these aspects form the contradictions of her life and work. As Clare Hanson points out, "as a writer Katherine Mansfield produced no single magnum opus. Consequently, there is no obvious focus for assessing her achievement or even for identifying her distinctive qualities."[7] However, *The Complete Stories of Katherine Mansfield*[8] and *Undiscovered Country: The New Zealand Stories of Katherine Mansfield*[9] along with her *Journals*, *Letters* and *Critical Writings* leave no room for any doubt about her eminence as a Commonwealth writer.

II

We may begin with two statements by Mansfield herself, one about her life and the other about the short story form:

> My literary career began with short story writing in New Zealand. I was nine years old when my first attempt was published. I have been filling notebooks eversince. After I came to London I worked for some time for the NEW AGE, and published IN A GERMAN PENSION in 1912. It was a bad book, but the press was kind to it. Later, I worked with my present husband, Mr. John Middleton Murry, editor of THE ATHENEUM, but at that time editor of RHYTHM and THE BLUE REVIEW. In the past two years I have reviewed novels for THE ATHENEUM and I have written more short stories.[10]

Regarding the short story form, she writes:

> Suppose we put it in the form of a riddle. "I am neither a short story, nor a sketch, nor an impression, nor a tale. I am written in prose. I am a great deal shorter than a novel; I may be only one page long, but on the other hand, there is no reason why I should not be thirty. I have a special quality--a something, a something which is immediately perfectly recognizable. It belongs to me; it is of my essence. In fact I am often given away in the first sentence. I seem almost to stand or fall by it. It is to me what the first phase of the song is to the singer."[11]

These two statements again reinforce the fact that "her life and her fiction were tightly interlocked" and that "in her case, fiction and autobiography form a single indivisible opus." Since her "opus" and her achievement is in the field of the short story, in the interests of brevity and focus, only a single story of hers which is totally representative of Katherine Mansfield will be discussed here. The story is "Je ne parle pas Francais."

III

Mansfield's own description-- "I am neither a short story, nor a sketch, nor an impression, nor a tale" applies perfectly to "Je ne parle pas Francais." As Clare Hanson has pointed out:

> "Je ne parle pas Francais" is difficult to approach without some knowledge of its biographical circumstances. When Middleton Murry claimed that it contained a personal symbolism only he could understand, he was no doubt thinking about more of its features than the resemblance of Raoul Duquette to Francis Carco, the French writer with whom Katherine Mansfield had enjoyed an escapade three years before, in 1915. "The fate of the Mouse, caught in the toils of world's evil, abandoned by her lover," wrote Murry, "is Katherine's fate." . . . The autobiographical elements are far more thoroughly diffused through the story than is admitted in Murry's plain equation of Katherine with the Mouse.[12]

While this clearly establishes the "biographical" context for this prose narrative, it also illustrates the "symbolic method" of Katherine Mansfield which makes her a "modern" writer. It must be noticed that

> in a Mansfield story almost every detail has a symbolic as well as a narrative function. The details, or images, are intended to work in concert to create a mood or evoke a theme which is never directly stated. These oblique and indirect stories must thus be read with the same close responsiveness as a Symbolist or Modernist poem, if the full effect is to be realized.[13]

"Je ne parle pas Francais" is a collage of a series of images--"images that fresh images beget." "Je ne parle pas Francais" (which means "I do not speak French") which forms the "Refrain" in the story is the result of a mood of dejection, utter tiredness and also nostalgia. As she herself puts it in her letter of March 28, 1918, it speaks of her situation in Paris--that of "une Anglais in a predicament. . . . Je suis tres fatiguee."[14] In Katherine Mansfield's description of what a short story is, she said: "In fact I am often given away in the first sentence." The first two sentences of "Je ne parle pas Francais" are: "I do not know why I have such a fancy for this little cafe. It's dirty and sad, sad." (63) This opening "gives away" the essence of the story. The dominant mood of sadness was the result of the contrast between her suffering in Bandol and her happiness there two years before which was tragic in its irony. It was in this mood that "Je ne parle pas" was written. In her letter of January 3, 1918, she wrote to Murry:

> I really feel I OUGHT to send you some boughs and songs, for never was time nor place more suited, but to tell you the truth I am pretty well absorbed in what I am writing.[15]

On March 27, 1918, she wrote:

> This is a funny little café where I come to write you my forlorn, forlorn, letter. . . . There's such a pretty girl in this

> Café--a girl whom you would admire--and the man and woman who keep it, too are YOUR SORT. There are also some red carnations, a white dog and a yellow basket covered in a red and white fringed cloth. It would be very beautiful if I were in the least alive. But I am not.[16]

"Je ne parle pas Francais" is a very special story of Katherine Mansfield for a number of reasons, including for the present context of Tradition and Modernity. Both from the point of view of subject matter as well as the narrative technique it is unique--as unique as the personality of its author. The "personal symbolism" that Murry saw in it has already been referred to. The bold representation of her own sex-life in her stories in general and in this story in particular reminds one of D.H. Lawrence's view of her as a "destructive witch-like figure, ultimately apotheosis, if that be the word," as Gudrun in *Women in Love*.[17] Of course, the contrary perspective of her as a saint has been given by Murry. The roles that he played in her life as a husband as well as her literary mentor often intersect. Role playing is crucial to any discussion of Katherine Mansfield as she herself consciously and constantly indulged in role playing. That is why the myth and reality about the "personality" which Mansfield was could only end up in the realization that she was an enigma. This enigmatic character, the present writer would like to suggest, was the result of the conflict between Tradition and Modernity in her life as well as in her art as the two are inseparable in her case. As a "colonial" from New Zealand she was brought up in a "traditional" suburban setting as a girl. The determination to be an artist impelled her from within to break away from tradition and convention to which a woman of her time was confined to. In this sense she is a "modern" and a rebel. When once she came to the Metropolis, London, her whole life underwent a metamorphosis. Within four years from 1908,

> She had several love-affairs and many transient jobs. A miscarriage in a forlorn village in Bavaria, an abortion and her one-day marriage were among the consequences of the love-affairs. Acting, including dancing in a chorus line in Liverpool and working in several casual jobs for which she felt qualified by her early training for a musical career,

were amongst her other experiences.[18]

These personal details have been given here to argue that Katherine Mansfield was a rebel against tradition, an advocate of feminism and a precursor and pioneer of the women's liberation movement. Her "modernity" in art took the form of experimenting with the new "plotless" story of which "Je ne parle pas" is an example. While her stories like "Pictures," "Mr. Reginald Peacock's Day" and "A Dill Pickle" have a "story" of sorts, her "Prelude," "Je ne parle pas Francais," "The Man Without a Temperament," "Psychology," "The Wind Blows," "The Escape," "Revelations," "Feuille D'Album" are stories in what has been termed as the "symbolist" mode. Though "Je ne parle pas," "The Man Without a Temperament" and "Psychology" are all based on Katherine Mansfield's relationship with Murry and are thus "autobiographical," "Je ne parle pas Francais" has been something special to its author. It is an epitome of Katherine Mansfield--which proves Isherwood's comment that "in her case, fiction and autobiography form a signle indivisible opus." To recollect Mansfield on the short story, "I may be only one page long, but on the other hand, there is no reason why I should not be thirty. . . . It belongs to me; it is of my essence." "Je ne parle pas" is indeed just a little longer than thirty pages--in the Penguin edition anyway--and it certainly "belongs" to her. It is of her "essence." That is why she seemed to be very fond of that story. If one reads the entries in her *Journal* and comments and notes on it in her *Letters* at the time she was working on it, one is left in no doubt about its importance in her ouvre. Take for example two entries in her *Journal*:

> C'est de la misere. Non, pas ca exactment. Il y a quelque chose--une profonde malaise me suive comme un ombre.[19]
>
> The Cafe was all but deserted. Over in the corner there sat a poor little creature with two loops of velvet in her hat that gave her the look of a rabbit. She was writing a letter. First she wrote a little, and then she looked up, and the two bows of ribbon seemed to pout, to listen. Then she crouched down again and scribbled another sheet. Again she looked up. The foxy waiter had his eye on her.[20]

While the first quotation establishes the context of sadness and misery in the story, the second gives us a sample of the vignettes that constitute the story "Je ne parle pas."

IV

"Je ne parle pas Francais" is a narrative in the first person. The narrator Raoul Duquette is the personification of the "free artist" in the Bohemian Paris. In this self portrait of Duquette are incorporated other persons, Dick and Mouse. In the dramatic monologue technique that has been used here, the narrator and the narrative merge. The story is composed of a series of misunderstandings, reluctant connections and blurred communications. The tone is set by the way the narrator introduces himself:

> My name is Raoul Duquette. I am twenty six years old and a Parisian, a true Parisian. About my family--it really doesn't matter; I don't want any. I never think about my childhood. I've forgotten it. (68)

The story explores the "ménage a trois" situation with a difference--through a very delicately woven web of the magical string so characteristic of the art of Katherine Mansfield. The story ends not with a bang but a whimper:

> Yes, you're very kind. Yes, do come tomorrow. I shall be glad. It makes things rather difficult because--and again I clasped her boyish hand--"je ne parle pas Francais."
>
> Not until I was half way down the boulevard did it come over me--the full force of it.
>
> Why, they were suffering . . . those two . . . really suffering. I have seen two people suffer as I don't suppose I ever shall again. . . . Je ne parle pas Francais. That was her swan song for me. (93)

It is difficult to determine to what extent this autobiographical story involving him and Francis Carco influenced Middleton Murry's attempts to edit the work. Katherine Mansfield herself was furious that any attempt should be made to alter the slightest detail in the story. In her letter of April 6, 1920 to Murry, she wrote:

> I've just got your note about "Je ne parle pas." No, I certainly won't agree to those excisions if there were 500,000,000 copies in existence. They can keep their old £ 40 and be hanged to them. Shall I pick the eyes out of a story for £ 40. I am furious. No, I shall never agree.[21]

However, there is a difference in the ending between the original text as published by the Heron Press (1919) and the Constable version. Clare Hanson is of the opinion that "it is clear that Murry had a hand in the bowdlerisation of K.M's fiction."[22] She gives the two additional paragraphs that are found in the original text and comments:

> I must go. I must go. I reach down my coat and hat. Madame knows me. "You haven't dined yet?" she smiles. "No, not yet, Madame." [Constable text ends here.]
>
> I'd rather like to dine with her. Even to sleep with her afterwards. Would she be pale like that all over?
>
> But no, she'd have large moles. They go with that kind of skin. And I can't bear them. They remind me somehow, disgustingly, of mushrooms.
>
> Many references to sexuality (important for the particular kind of "corruption" KM was evoking here) have been cut out for the Constable editon: KM felt she had "picked the eyes out of [her] story" at Murry's and Michael Sadleir's instigation, to ensure its publication. Of course, she was responding to social pressures, not only to Murry, in doing this, and it would be wrong to suggest that Murry should take sole responsibility.[23]

This last bit has been quoted to make the point that Katherine Mansfield was breaking away from the Victorian notions of tradition--the way a woman writer should write and she was ushering in the era of modernity--rebelling against conventional ideas of prudery and "propriety."

V

Coming from a traditional colonial bourgeois home in New Zealand, Katherine Mansfield took to "modern" ideas and ways in Europe. This can be seen in two areas which in her case, as has been pointed out at the beginning, became one and indistinguishable--her life and her art. Though critics have seen the influence of Chekhov on her writing, the first model that she took for the expression of her artistic personality was Oscar Wilde. Though she and Rudyard Kipling established their reputation on the short story form, it was Beatrice Hastings and feminist writing which served as her real inspiration and her technique is very different indeed from that of Kipling. As Clare Hanson and Andrew Gurr put it:

> It was through her (Beatrice Hastings) that Katherine Mansfield first came into contact with feminism as a genuine force, and through her that she was able to place her personal sense of conflict in a wider context. Under Beatrice Hastings' influence, she wrote several articles and stories for THE NEW AGE on feminist themes: for example, the uncollected "At the Club," "A Marriage of Passion," and "The Mating of Gwendolen." Many of her "Bavarian Sketches" in THE NEW AGE, later published in IN A GERMAN PENSION deal with the same issues: for instance, "At Lehmann's" and "From Brechenmacher Attends a Wedding." In these stories she explores the economic factors that may force women into marriage against their will, and also the widespread ignorance of sexual matters that led to so much stress and disillusion for women. Through her writing she thus relates her own rejection of the conventional married role to a wider historical and social background, and in so doing justifies her position, and her efforts towards freedom.[24]

As far as the modernity of her art is concerned, it is significant that T.S.Eliot, in his *After Strange Gods* looks at three short stories: Katherine Mansfield's "Bliss," Lawrence's "The Shadow in the Rose Garden" and Joyce's "The Dead" in his discussion of the modern temper. It is equally significant that Mansfield described "Prufrock" as "after all a short story" in a letter to Virginia Woolf.[25] Hanson points out:

> Two entirely different types of story flourished together at the close of the nineteenth century. First, there was the story with a definite plot, which was the lineal descendent of the Gothic tale; and second, there was the new, "plotless" story, concentrating on inner mood and impression rather than on external event. . . . Katherine Mansfield certainly saw her kind of story as a quintessentially modern form.[26]

To sum up this brief study of Katherine Mansfield, it is perhaps best to return to Christopher Isherwood's appraisal:

> Katherine Mansfield's life is so fascinating because despite its surface tangle of moods, impetuous reactions and rash decisions--it presents a very symbolic pattern. This is a variant of the Garden of Eden theme. A childhood paradise is lost. An apple of knowledge is eaten, with bitter consequences. And then under the curse and blessing of that knowledge, comes the attempt to regain the paradise. It is a deeply moving story.[27]

NOTES

1. Katherine Mansfield, "Je ne parle pas Francais," *Bliss and Other* Stories (Penguin, 1962), p. 63.
2. Christopher Isherwood, "Katherine Mansfield," *Exhumations* (Penguin, 1969), p. 81.
3. Clare Hanson and Andrew Gurr: *Katherine Mansfield* (Macmillan, 1981), p. 2.
4. *Journal of Katherine Mansfield*, ed. J. Middleton Murry (Definitive Edition, London: Constable, 1954).
5. *Katherine Mansfield's Letters to John Middleton Murry, 1913-1922*, ed. John Middleton Murry (London: Constable, 1951, Rep. 1958).
6. *The Critical Writings of Katherine Mansfield*, ed. and Intro.

Clare Hanson (Macmillan, 1987).

7. Hanson and Gurr, p. 14.
8. *The Complete Stories of Katherine Mansfield* (Auckland: Golden Press, 1978).
9. *Undiscovered Country: The New Zealand Stories of Katherine Mansfield*, ed. I.A. Gordon (Longman, 1974).
10. *Journal*, p. 252.
11. *The Critical Writings*, p. 99.
12. Hanson and Gurr. p. 65.
13. *Ibid.*, p. 22.
14. *Letters*, pp. 231-32.
15. *Letters*, p. 148.
16. *Ibid.*, p. 230.
17. Quoted by Hanson and Gurr, p. 2.
18. *Ibid.*, p. 5.
19. *Journal*, p. 138.
20. *Ibid.*, p. 242.
21. *Letters*, p. 515.
22. Hanson and Gurr, p. 3.
23. *Ibid.*, p. 4.
24. *Ibid.*, p. 12.
25. Quoted by Hanson and Gurr, p. 59.
26. *Ibid.*, pp. 17, 18.
27. Christopher Isherwood, p. 81.

Katherine Mansfield as a Short-Story Writer

INDIBAR MUKHERJEE

The displacement of plot is the chief element which, more than anything else, marks the modern short story as different from the type of story generally written before 1910. As plot is the ordering of action, there is not much of a plot in the modern short story, but instead we find the psychological reaction of the protagonist to a particular incident or incidents.

Katherine Mansfield is a modern short story writer like D.H. Lawrence. In her short stories we find psychology playing a vital role as in the stories of D.H. Lawrence. She, like Chekhov, presents one train of events and suggests another. She does not state but suggests. What she says and what she does not say are equally suggestive. Her short stories seem to tremble on the brink of poetry.

In "The Doll's House" Katherine Mansfield shows how the grown-up people vitiate the minds of innocent children by making them conscious of class distinctions.

Old Mrs. Hay sent a doll's house to the Burnell children as a gift. Isabel, Lottie and Kezia were delighted. Kezia liked particularly the lamp on the dining table in that doll's house. The doll's house was kept beside the feed-room door because Aunt Beryl thought that the smell of the paint would make anyone ill. The doll's house was painted spinach green but the doors were bright yellow.

At school Isabel told everyone about the doll's house. She was the eldest and so she had the right to talk first. She, however, did not mention the lamp. So Kezia pointed out that the lamp was the finest thing in the doll's house. Two girls, Lil and Else, listened to Isabel and Kezia from distance because they were the children of the washerwoman and nobody was allowed to talk to them. As there was only one school, all the children of the locality, rich and poor, read there, but the children of the upper class were forbidden to talk to those of the working class.

Isabel invited two children everyday to see the doll's house. Soon all the children were talking about the wonder. Poor Lil and Else heard everything but they knew that they were not to see the wonder.

Then one day Lena Logan insulted Lil by asking her if she would become a servant when she grew up. Everybody enjoyed the cruel remark.

That evening Kezia found Lil and Else coming up the road. She opened the gate and wanted to know if they would like to see the doll's house. Lil said that she was forbidden to speak to girls like Lil and Else. But Kezia insisted. Else pulled the dress of her sister signifying that she wanted to see the wonder. So Lil yielded. Lil and Else followed Kezia.

As they were watching the wonder, Aunt Beryl appeared and drove the poor girls away. She also took Kezia to task for talking to the washerwoman's daughters whose father was a prisoner.

Lil and Else sat on a big red drainpipe. They had forgotten the cross lady. Else said softly:

"I seen the little lamp."

The little lamp, admired by Kezia, was also a symbol of Kezia's innocence, sympathy and humanity. Lil and Else had not only seen the lamp, but also the lamp in Kezia.

This short story is remarkable for its psychological realism which shows how children react to class distinctions. Lena Logan and Kezia react differently. The former is cruel while the latter is sympathetic. The underdogs of the society, Lil and Else, behave differently too. Lil does not like to offend the upper classes but Else accepts the sympathy of Kezia.

"The Fly" is a deeply moving story of sorrow and mental anguish. It is marked by a relative absence of action and reveals a particular mood by the introduction of trivial incidents.

Mr. Woodifield, an old invalid, is allowed to come out of his house once a week. He is an old friend of the boss, the owner of a big firm. One day he pays a visit to the boss in his office. He praises the room where all the details have been specially arranged by the boss. He, however, cannot recall something that he wants to tell. The boss then brings out a bottle of wine and shares it with Mr. Woodifield. Then Mr. Woodifield remembers what he has to say. His daughters visited Belgium where they saw the grave of the only son of the boss. The young man had been killed in the First World War.

When Mr. Woodifield goes away, the boss feels that he must weep. Six years have passed since the death of his son. He had built up his huge business in the hope that his son would succeed him. But his hope was foiled. The young man was killed in Belgium. When the boss got the news, he felt that he would never get over the shock.

But six years after that incident the boss finds that tears do not flow. He wants to weep but cannot. Suddenly his attention is drawn to a fly in the inkpot. He helps the fly to come out. Then he places it on a piece of blotting-paper. The fly begins to struggle. The boss watches how the fly cleans its wings and gets ready to fly. He then covers the fly with a blot of ink. The fly struggles again and cleans its wings, but before it can fly the boss covers it with another blot of ink. It is now very weak, but it struggles and manages to free itself. Then the boss lets another blot of ink fall on the fly and kills it. A feeling of wretchedness and horror fills the boss. He throws the dead fly into the wastepaper basket. Then he rings the bell. When Macey appears he asks him to bring a fresh piece of blotting paper. He tries to remember what he was thinking about but fails.

The chain of events leading to the death of the fly suggests a parallel in human life. The boss is wretched and horrified because he realizes that he is like the fly. He has been struggling against the blow given by Fate. He has almost forgotten the sorrow caused by his son's death. But Fate has no mercy. Other blows will fall. Life is never daunted. Till death it goes on struggling like the fly. One may indict life because in course of time it forgets every sorrow. One may praise life at the same time for its tenacity. Katherine Mansfield suggests all these things by her Chekhov-like indirect method and her art of suppressing many details. The fly is a poetic symbol so that the story seems to tremble on the very brink of poetry.

"A Cup of Tea" is another story which seems to tremble on the brink of poetry, because of the subtle handling of the theme. It is a story about a happy couple Philip and Rosemary who had been married for two years and had a baby.

One winter evening Rosemary paid a visit to an antique shop in Curzon street and decided to buy a little box costing twenty-eight guineas. As she came out, a thin large-eyed girl came to her and prayed for the price of a cup of tea. Since Rosemary had read all the classics, she wanted to behave like one of the characters of Dostoevsky. So she brought the girl home and took her to her bed-room. There she served her tea, sandwiches and other delicacies. Rosemary felt that all women were sisters and so she wanted to be very kind to that poor girl. The girl gave out her name to be Miss Smith.

At this time Philip came in and observed the coat and the battered hat of the girl on the floor. Rosemary told him how she had picked Miss Smith up from the Curzon street. Philip then took his wife to the library and remarked that the girl was pretty and lovely. He wanted to know if she would stay for the dinner.

Rosemary took out three one-pound notes and went to her bedroom. After sometime she came back into the library to tell her husband that Miss Smith would not stay for the dinner and so she had given her some money out of kindness. Then she went close to her husband and wanted to know if she was pretty. Her husband answered her that she was.

It is clear that Philip wanted to get rid of the poor girl and so he called her pretty. He knew well that this would make Rosemary jealous. His trick worked. Rosemary's kindness, sense of equality and sisterly feeling gave way to a sense of rivalry. So she got rid of Miss Smith.

The rainy evening and Rosemary's bedroom are presented with suggestive touches. The whole story is beautiful and delicate like a poem. The ultimate picture is that of conjugal love and family bliss.

In this way we see that Katherine Mansfield though born in New Zealand and brought up in Europe has got a universal appeal because of her timeless themes. These short stories can be appreciated at any time and at any place.

"Like a Child with a Box of Bricks": Katherine Mansfield's New Zealand Stories

RADHARANI CHAKRAVARTY

"I thank God I was born in New Zealand. A young country is a real heritage, though it takes one time to recognize it."[1] In these words, written a few months before her death, Katherine Mansfield acknowledges her debt to her birthplace, from which she had voluntarily exiled herself before she was twenty. Mansfield's attitude towards New Zealand remained ambivalent to the end of her life, but there is no doubt that her early experiences in this country played a major role in her development as an artist.

After her exposure to life at Queen's College, London, Katherine Mansfield rebelled against what she regarded as the restrictiveness of New Zealand society. "Talk of our enlightened days and our emancipated country--pure nonsense! We are firmly held with the self-fashioned chains of slavery. Yes, now I see that they *are* self-fashioned, and must be self-removed." (*LJ*, 35) Back in London in 1908, she again found herself a misfit, and alienation became one of the recurring themes of her stories. "I am the little Colonial walking in the London garden-patch--allowed to look, perhaps, but not to linger. If I lie on the grass, they positively shout at me: 'Look at her, lying on *our* grass, pretending she lives here. . . She is a stranger--an alien. She is nothing but a little girl sitting on the Tinakori hills and dreaming.'"[2]

Although she spent the rest of her life in England and Europe, Katherine Mansfield was never really able to shake off the influence of her early days in New Zealand. After the death of her brother in 1915, she returned passionately to her memories of this period, which provided her with material for some of her finest stories. "I want to write recollections of my own country. . . . Oh, I want for one moment to make our undiscovered country leap into the eyes of the Old World." (*LJ*, 65) The world she creates in her New Zealand stories is "undiscovered country," because what she seeks to capture is the spirit of the land, its elusive essence: "It must be mysterious, as though floating."

In the poem *To Stanislaw Wyspianski* (1910), Mansfield describes New Zealand as

> a little land with no history,
> (Making its own history, slowly and clumsily
> Piecing together this and that, finding the
> patterns solving the problem,
> Like a child with a box of bricks) (*LJ*, 39)

New Zealand is seen as a "young" nation in a state of innocence that is almost prelapserian, but the picture is shot with an ironic awareness of the limitations of such an existence.

> My people have had nought to contend with;
> They have worked in the broad light of day
> and handled the clay with rude fingers;
> Life--a thing of blood and muscle; Death--
> a shovelling underground of waste material. . . .
> Fine and sweet the water that runs from their mountains;
> How could they know of poisonous weed, of rotted and clogging tendrils?

Simplicity here borders on crudity and ignorance. The people of New Zealand, with their "stupid hands" and "childish laughter," are not subtle enough to cope with the darker side of life. The new country, with its abundant and contradictory energies, provides Mansfield with an analogue for herself, as the young woman artist struggling to achieve a sense of her own identity:

> I, a woman with the taint of the pioneer in my blood
> Full of a youthful strength that wars with itelf and is lawless. . . .

This parallel provides the basis for the complex exploration of childhood experiences in her New Zealand stories.

Life in New Zealand is rarely romanticized in Katherine Mansfield's works. In "The Woman at the Store," the bleakness of the setting provides an ominous backdrop to the tale of murder in the colonial backblocks: "There is no twilight in our New Zealand days, but a curious half-hour when everything appears grotesque--it frightens--as though the savage spirit of the country walked abroad and sneered at what it saw."[3] Social life, in the stories of the Burnells and the Sheridans, is characterized by conservatism and class-consciousness. In "At the Bay" (1921), the unconventional behaviour of Mrs. Harry Kember provides food for local gossip: "The women at the bay thought she was very, very fast. Her lack of vanity, her slang, the way she treated men as though she was one of them, and the fact that she didn't care twopence about the house and called the servant Gladys 'Glad-eyes,' was disgraceful." (119) In "The Doll's House" (1921), Kezia's act of inviting the Kelveys to her house is treated as a violation of social hierarchy. It is unthinkable that the death of a cottager should interfere with the festivities of the Sheridan family in "The Garden Party" (1921).

Clearly, Mansfield's New Zealand stories are not mere studies in nostalgia. They are, in fact, a way of coming to terms with past experience, in such a way as to make it serve the present. "We only live by somehow absorbing the past--changing it. I mean really examining it and dividing what is important from what is not (for there IS waste) and transforming it so that it becomes part of the life of the spirit and we are *free of it*. It's no longer our personal past, it's just in the highest possible sense, our servant." (*LJ*, 192) Many of Mansfield's characters are based on real-life figures. Stanley Burnell, for example, is a fictional version of her own father, Sir Harold Beauchamp, while Linda Burnell is modelled on her frail, enigmatic mother, Annie. Tui, in "Kezia and Tui" is a version of Katherine's Maori classmate Maata at Miss Swainson's school. But in the process of being transformed into fictional characters, these figures from real life undergo a metamorphosis that makes it impossible to read the stories as simple autobiography. Embedded in the fictional matrix of Mansfield's stories, these characters acquire identities independent of their origin in their author's life.

The desire to transcend the personal underlies, also, Mansfield's habit of adopting a variety of "masks": "I think there is a very profound distinction between any kind of *confession* and creative work." (*LJ*, 190) Like her contemporary, Virginia Woolf, Katherine Mansfield seeks to efface herself from her work, by merging her creative self with that of her fictional characters. In a letter to John Middleton Murry, she describes how "The Stranger" was composed: "I've *been* this man, *been* this woman. I've stood for hours on the Auckland Wharf. I've been out in the stream waiting to be berthed--I've been a seagull hovering at the stern and a porter whistling through his teeth. It isn't as though one sits and watches the spectacle. That would be thrilling enough, God knows. But one IS the spectacle for the time." (3 Nov. 1920; *LJ*, 199) This ability to assume an infinite variety of roles is not only a version of the modernist concept of the fragmented self; it is also the woman artist's strategy for demonstrating the elusiveness and endless flexibility of the female self. The notion of identity as something fixed and definable is thus rejected in favour of a more radical conception of the self.

Mansfield's New Zealand stories, instead of promoting the traditional idea of unity, expose the tensions and disjunctions that characterize all human experience. In these stories, the self is at odds with its environment, with other people, and even with itself. The image of the fractured self emerges with particular force in "Prelude" (1915-17) and "At the Bay," both at one time intended as part of the projected novel *Karori*.

"Prelude," written after the traumatic loss of her brother Leslie in 1915, is based on Katherine Mansfield's memories of the time when her own family had moved from Wellington to Karori. In twelve carefully constructed sections, the story offers glimpses of the inner lives of the different characters, captured during this significant period of change and dislocation. The point of view shifts constantly, creating an almost post-modern decentring of the narrative through the gradual building up of a "polyphony of voices."

Initially, the child's-eye vision of Kezia and Lottie prevails: "Now everything familiar was left behind. Now the big dray rattled into unknown country, along roads with high clay banks on either side, up steep, steep hills, down into bushy valleys, through wide shallow rivers. Further and further." (35) In section IV, we hear the "voice" of Beryl, in a state of reverie: "A young man, immensely rich, has just arrived from England. He meets her quite by chance. . . . The new governor is unmarried. . . . There is a ball at Government house. . . . Who is that exquisite creature in eau-de-nil satin? Beryl Fairfield." (40) In section V, Linda's dream about her father is followed immediately by the "voice" of Stanley: "He was enormously pleased. Weather like this set a final seal on his bargain. He felt, somehow, that he had bought the lovely day, too--got it chucked in dirt cheap with the house and ground." (42) The juxtaposition of the "voices" of Linda and Stanley demonstrates their mental incompatibility more effectively than any authorial comment could have achieved. The short story writer does not always have the space to elaborate upon relationships in detail. Katherine Mansfield overcomes this difficulty by her clever manipulation of the "point of view," allowing these brief glimpses of the inner lives of her characters to suggest the discordant emotions that surge beneath the surface of daily domestic life.

Linda's resentment of Stanley stems from her rejection of sexuality and motherhood: "If only he wouldn't jump at her so, and bark so loudly, and watch her with such eager, loving eyes. He was too strong for her, she had always hated things that rushed at her, from a child." (67) There are undercurrents of tension between Beryl and Alice, the maid: "But what Alice really hated Miss Beryl for was that she made her feel low. She talked to Alice in a special voice as though she wasn't quite all there." (63) Beneath the placid surface of family life, horror and violence are never far away. The innocence and security of childhood is suddenly violated by the killing of a bird. "Put head back! Put head back!" screams Kezia, (61) unable to accept the brutal finality of death.

The fantasies of Linda and Beryl are indications of the subconscious urges that contradict the logic of everyday life. In Linda's dream, the trauma of childbearing is projected in the nightmare image of "a baby with a big naked head and a gaping bird-mouth, opening and shutting." (42) Beryl's awakening into sexuality is expressed in her private fantasy: "her breath rose and fell in her breast like two fanning wings. The window was wide open; it was warm, and somewhere out there in the garden a young man, dark and slender, with mocking eyes, tiptoed among the bushes, and gathered the flowers into a big bouquet, and slipped under her window and held it up to her." (40)

At significant moments in the story, Mansfield's characters become aware of the fragmented, incohesive nature of the self. Gazing at the symbolic aloe, Linda recognizes that her feelings for Stanley are by no means simple: "For all her love and respect and admiration she hated him. . . . She could have done her feelings up in little packets and given them to Stanley." (67-68) Beryl is tormented by the falseness of her own public self: "'oh', she cried, 'I am so miserable--so frightfully miserable. I know that I'm silly and spiteful and vain; I'm always acting a part. I'm never my real self for a moment'" (71) Beryl's anguished cry anticipates Katherine Mansfield's own journal entry in April 1920: "True to oneself! which self? Which of my many--well really, that's what it looks like coming to--hundreds of selves?" (*LJ,* 173)

Fragmentation creates a craving for unity and continuity: "Is it not possible that the rage for confession, autobiography, especially for memories of earliest childhood, is explained by our persistent yet mysterious belief in a self which is continuous and permanent?" (*LJ,* 173) This, perhaps, is the urge behind Mansfield's evocation of her own childhood memories in the New Zealand stories. Yet, in story after story, the illusion of permanence is shattered by sudden, "epiphanic" encounters with reality.

In "At the Bay," for example, there are a number of crucial moments when the characters suddenly become self-aware. Kezia, in a casual conversation with her grandmother, unexpectedly confronts the fact of death:

> "Does everybody have to die?" asked Kezia.
> "Everybody!"
> "*Me*?" Kezia sounded fearfully incredulous.
> "Someday, my darling." (126)

Kezia's frenzied cry, "Say never . . . say never . . . say never," echoes her trauma at the butchering of the duck in "Prelude."

Linda, who resents her role as a mother and feels biologically trapped, feels the sudden awakening of her maternal instinct as she watches her baby's confident demand for attention: "it was something far different, it was something so new, so. . . The tears danced in her eyes; she breathed in a small whisper to the boy, 'Hallo, my funny!'" (123)

Beryl, stifled by the conservative atmosphere at Crescent Bay, is tempted by Mrs. Harry Kember's offer of liberation through defiance of convention. But at night, stealing out for a secret rendezvous with Harry Kember, Beryl is checked by a sudden flash of perception: "that bright, blind, terrifying smile froze her with horror. What was she doing? How had she got here?" (142) She instantly changes her mind and escapes, leaving Harry bewildered and alone: "Then why in God's name did you come?"

The moment of "epiphany" occurs also in "The Garden Party," when Laura, in the midst of a party, learns of the death of a man living nearby. Confronted with the absurdity of life, she struggles inarticulately to communicate her insight to her brother, Laurie: "'Isn't life,' she stammered, 'isn't life--' But what life was she couldn't explain. No matter. He quite understood." (227) In "The Doll's House," the vision of the lamp momentarily unites Kezia and Else, spanning the social gulf which separates them. The "boss" in "The Fly" (1922) faces a moment of terror after his arbitrary destruction of a harmless insect: "such a grinding feeling of wretchedness seized him that he felt positively frightened. He started forward." (296) In a journal entry dated February 1920, Mansfield tries to articulate the significance of such moments of awareness: "What is it that happens in that moment of suspension? It is timeless. In that moment . . . the whole life of the soul is contained. One is flung up--out of life--one is 'held,' and then--down, bright, broken, glittering on to the rock, tossed back, part of the ebb and flow." (*LJ*, 169-70)

Towards the end of her life, suffering from terminal illness, Katherine Mansfield was increasingly tormented by the shadow of death. "At the Bay," though modelled on "Prelude," is much more sombre than the earlier story. The human drama takes place against a hauntingly evoked backdrop of sea and sky, symbolizing the cycle of birth and death that must be accepted. Here, as in "Prelude," tensions and disjunctions operate powerfully beneath the surface. Stanley Burnell, the epitome of order, convention and hierarchy, is blind to the strain he places upon his family, who must be at his beck and call to ensure that his morning routine remains undisturbed. When he leaves, the women experience a shared sense of freedom: "Oh, the relief, the difference it made to have the man out of the house. Their very voices were changed as they called to one another; they sounded warm and loving and as if they shared a secret." (115) Kezia fights knowledge of death; Linda struggles with the demands of motherhood; Beryl chafes against the bonds of her sheltered existence. These tensions are not resolved; choices (between motherhood and selfhood for Linda, between promiscuity and sobriety for Beryl) are not simple. Questions remain unanswered. When, at the end of the story, Harry Kember demands an explanation from Beryl, he is answered only by silence and the sound of the sea: "a vague murmur, as though it waked out of a dark dream. All was still." (142)

Paradoxically, the knowledge of death only made Katherine Mansfield more passionately aware of the beauty of life. "And yes, that is what I tried to convey in 'The Garden Party.' The diversity of life and how we try to fit in everything. Death included . . . it is inevitable. And it seems to me there is beauty in that inevitability." (*LJ*, 259) Of all Mansfield's characters, it is perhaps Mrs. Fairfield, Kezia's grandmother, who comes closest to recognizing and accepting this inevitable complexity. In harmony with her surroundings and in tune with nature, she is almost mythified as a source of comfort for the troubled people around her. Linda, watching her mother in the kitchen, "thought her mother looked wonderfully beautiful with her back to the leafy window. There was something comforting in the sight of her that Linda felt she could never do without." (48) The peace and repose that characterize Mrs. Fairfield stem from her ability to accept all the contradictions inherent in the pattern of life and death.

"Life is not simple," declares Mansfield. "In spite of all we say about the mystery of Life, when we get down to it we want to treat it as though it were a child's tale." (*LJ*, 278) Childhood experiences fascinate her, but in the best of her New Zealand stories, she resists the temptation to romanticize and oversimplify. Because of Mansfield's refusal to gloss over contradictions, her stories do not furnish neat answers to fundamental questions about life and death. Their strength resides, instead, in the cogency with which these vital questions are articulated.

NOTES

1. Katherine Mansfield, letter to Sir Harold Beauchamp, 18 March 1922, *The Letters and Journals of Katherine Mansfield: A Selection*, ed. C.K. Stead (London: Allen Lane, 1977), p. 260. Abbreviated as *LJ*.
2. Katherine Mansfield, *Journal*, ed. John Middleton Murry (1954; New York: McGraw Hill, 1964), p. 157.
3. *Undiscovered Country: The New Zealand Stories of Katherine Mansfield*, ed. Ian A. Gordon (Bristol: Longman, 1974), p. 340.

Human Relationships in the Stories of Frank Sargeson

VEENA NOBLE DASS

Bonds of trade and kinship tied New Zealand so firmly to Britain that it was long considered as the Britain of the South Pacific. Although it ceased to be a colony in 1907, another forty years passed before it set up its own foreign ministry and began to develop an independent foreign policy. Nearly ninety per cent of its people are of European origin and English is the most widely spoken language. New Zealander's customs and social structure remain essentially British.

An important feature of New Zealand's new society is the recent increase in the number of Maoris--the Polynesians who inhabited the islands for at least 700 years before the first European Dutchman Abel Tarman and his crew saw them in 1642.[1]

In all its interests the country knows no class or colour barriers. Ever since the days of the first settlers when New Zealanders found that social divisions did not help to form the land, society has been fair and perhaps uniquely classless. Most of the writers project this classless society in their writings. Three of the most distinguished contemporary New Zealand writers--Frank Sargeson, Dan Davin and Janet Frame--have each continued to make substantial contributions each to his own "oeuvre" and all to the literature of the country.

In a colonial situation where English middle class social values are inappropriate, the first really belivable characters in fiction are usually the eccentrics and outcasts. It was Frank Sargeson who made such types, representative of an authentic New Zealand. Sargeson's grandparents emigrated to New Zealand in the 1870s. He studied law, qualified as a solicitor and worked in law office until 1927 when he left for England and Europe where he travelled, read widely and tried to write an autobiographical novel. Increasingly aware that England was not "home" and that there he was an alien, Sargeson returned to the New Zealand from which he had previously fled because of its puritanism, conformity and lack of culture. He worked briefly in a government department but after a mental collapse he decided to give up any attempt to live a conventional, respectable life. Although it would mean a break with his family, he decided to be a writer and began studying the problem in adapting the craft of fiction to the circumstances of local life. While for a short time during the 1930s Sargeson belonged to the Communist Party, he quickly rebelled against its discipline.

Sargeson follows a pattern often noticeable in commonwealth writers: rebellion against a stodgy middle class background, expatriation, discovery abroad that one is not British, return to the native land both as a critic of its colonial bourgeoisie and with a new awareness of it as home.

During the 1930s and 40s Sargeson worked towards creating a fictional style appropriate for his country. The result was a small body of sketches and short stories in which language, subject, attitude, characters and form capture representative qualities of New Zealand life. Drawing upon the depression concern with the down and out, the out of work, the poor, he wrote realistically of the attitudes and world of the social underdog, the disappointed immigrant, the drifters, wanderers and rootless. While the stories imply sympathy and compassion, the tone is flat, objective and tinged with irony in comparison to the idealizing of the poor, often found in "protest" writing. The stories often indirectly attack the middle class and capitalism by quietly bringing into prominence callousness. exploitation and social conformity.

The social disorder resulting from an underpopulated underprivileged settler society is reflected in the episodic lives of his fictional characters and in the anecdotal nature of his stories. He captured the then often remarked upon isolated, improvised quality of local life, especially among the labourers in the small towns and on the farm. It is a society in which men are equal but without communal bonds, an atomized society in which the "mate," a companion of the same sex, temporarily becomes what equivalent there is of the family. The language of the stories is idiomatic, the vocabulary has many local words, rhythms of speech and sentence patterns give the impression of typical New Zealand talk.

My paper deals, in some detail, two of Sargeson's stories--"That Summer" and "A Man and His Wife"--in which the above-mentioned characteristics of his art specially of human relationship are found. "That Summer" is an attempt at capuring within the apparently casual joining up of two "mates" an analogous relationship to that more often associated with an intense, shattering doomed love affair between a man and a woman.

The story is as follows. Although during the depression jobs are almost unobtainable, Billy the narrator quits his employment, goes to town, tries to "pick up with a girl" and rents a room in a boarding house where husband and wife "squabble." He meets, treats to dinner, goes to the movies, and gets drunk with a casual acquaintance named Sam. He is free with the little money he has. Besides paying for Sam, he drops coins around a tree where his landlord's child can find them and shrugs it off when another casual acquaintance, Ted, robs him of his remaining money. "What's money anyhow, I thought." Bill survives on odd jobs, trickery, petty thievery and betting on races. He becomes mates with Terry, another of the unemployed, with whom he shares a room. Unlike the quarrelling husbands and wives of Sargeson's stories, Bill and Terry seem to get along through some unspoken man to man code. They undergo various adventures in trying to survive, the point of which illustrates "A man wants a mate that won't let him down, he said." Bill is seduced by Maggie, who tells people that he raped her. After being imprisoned, awaiting trial, he is freed when Maggie is frightened by Terry into withdrawing her complaint. When he comes out of prison, Bill finds that Terry has been put in hospital because of his bad lungs and is unable to walk. He manages to sneak him from the hospital and takes him back to his room in the boarding house where he cares for him until he dies.

The penultimate paragraph of the story stands in sharp contrast to that various quarrelling and anguished relationships portrayed between men and women, and is an excellent example of Sargeson's craftsmanship:

I'd look at him lying there.

Terry, I'd say.

What is it boy? he'd say.

Nothing, I'd say

And then I'd say, Terry.

And instead of answering he'd just have a sort of faint grin on his face.

Terry, I'd say.

But I never could get any further than just saying Terry. I wanted to say something but I didn't know what it was and I couldn't say it.

Terry, I'd say.

And he'd sort of grin. And sometimes I'd take his hand and hold it tight, and he'd let it stay in my hand, and there'd be the faint grin on his face.

Terry, I'd say.

I'm all right boy, he'd say.

And sometimes I couldn't stand it, I'd have to just rush off and leave him there.

And one night when I came back again I looked at him and knew it was the finish.

Terry, I said, and he didn't answer.

Terry, I said, and I said I was going to get the priest.

Cheers boy, is what I think he said, and I rushed off without even saying goodbye.[2]

The repetitions, the dependence on the notation of inarticulateness and the intrinsic sentimentalism reveal the limitations of Sargeson's method and sensibility.

Similar characteristics are found in his other story *A Man and His Wife*.[3] Ted, the protagonist, baulked from finding an outlet for his feelings in his marriage, is forced to find some form of emotional release by keeping at first a dog which is killed and then a canary. The depth of his feelings when he loses even that and returns to his wife is merely implied in the flat exchange of remarks with which the story concludes:

"I've still got the wife," he said

"Yes" I said

"The wife never let me down," he said.

"No" I said. (121)

Like Hemingway's characters, Sargeson's are inarticulate men, not without feelings, but unable to express themselves. The limitations of their understanding is demarcated by the limits of their speech. Like Ted and the narrator of this story, they often feel an instinctive but tacit comradeship with each other, similar to the "mateship" that is also found in Australian life and literature especially in Henry Lawson's work.[4] But whereas for the Australian men in the outback, mateship was an answer to the loneliness of the vast solitudes surrounding them on all sides, in Sargeson's work solitude is a state of mind. It is the hardship of their lives that brings his characters together as we see in these lines:

> Along the street you'd meet too many who were as hard put to it as you were yourself. (118)

And it is also this relationship which helps alleviate these conditions:

> that's one thing the slump did, it put a certain sort of comradeship into life that you don't find now. (118)

As the tone indicates, however, this is not a bond of personal relationship that is idealized in any way. Sargeson is too much of a realist, too aware of some of the conditions of modern man whether in New Zealand or elsewhere, for that to happen. If his characters can become "cobbers" they can also drift apart again as casually as they do in this story, leaving them alone and rootless in a New Zealand and in a country of the mind where, even while they are at home, they are still inescapably solitary and alien.

While Sargeson is one of the best writers of short stories within the new national literatures, there are obvious limitations to the conventions and techniques he has found useful to describe New Zealand life--naive narrators and extreme reliance on colloquial speech and social underdogs. Such writing is at first liberating from the English novel of manners or novel of ideas but suffers from many of the same handicaps as local colour sketches, folk tales and frontier stories. It cannot respond to the texture of settled society, record subtleties of manner and sensibility, examine the intricacies of public power or the complexities of human desire. Yet Sargeson speaks from an authentic and now confidently settled New Zealand sensibility and keeps alive the unique note of New Zealand's contribution to the literature of the English language.

NOTES

1. *Guide to Places of the World* (London: The Reader's Digest Association, 1987).
2. Bruce King, *The New English Literatures* (London: Macmillan, 1980), p. 148.
3. Anna Rutherford and Donald Hannah, ed., *Commonwealth Short Stories* (London: Edward Arnold, 1971), pp. 118-21.
4. *Ibid.*, p. 117.

A Rhetoric of Sentiment: Thoughts on Maori Writing with reference to the Short-Stories of Witi Ihimaera

PAUL SHARRAD

Reading a critique of fiction by the Maori writer, Witi Ihimaera, I was again struck by the dilemma of the Eurocentric critic who attempts an evaluation of literature by people whose cultures have roots in what White history has termed "primitive" or non-modern cultures. Typical responses can be reduced to two general kinds. Firstly, there is the search to see how well the writer conveys a sense of his/her socio-cultural milieu. (Often this background is defined according to the critic's stereotyped view of the minority culture as a museum artefact, something exotic, a fresh resource for the Literature Factory, vital and novel, but also to be handled with care and labelled "rare," "old" or both.) Secondly, there is the effort to judge the new work according to some hypothetical standard of European genre conventions and language-use.

In Ihimaera's case, critics have looked for a creative manipulation of English that respects the "integrity" of the language, and for innovations that allow the introduction of new content (new conceptions of character, different ways of perceiving the passage of time through narrative, unusual social relationships etc.) and a "new ethical feeling for man's place in the natural world." None of these changes are permitted to flout the laws of literary tradition, however, without attracting censure. It all has an air of the tired Westerner indulging in Romantic yearnings for redemption through an infusion of primitive oneness with Nature. But, like the Romantics, our critics seem only to want a tameable kind of energy, fighting shy of the revolutionary otherness symbolized in Draculas, Ayeshas and assorted

Hearts of Darkness.

As a consequence, the demands placed on minority writing are extreme and frequently contradictory. Especially if the literature finds expression in the majority (or dominant) language, it is not enough for the writer to want to speak to his/her own community; to gain the reputation that is often associated with achieving cultural visibility and/or acceptance for the community, the writer has to be a success according to the Eurocentric standards of institutionalized literary debate. Ihimaera is charged, on the one hand, with the task of putting "his imagination firmly in harmony with the archetypal rhythms of Maori myth and ritual" and criticized for not conveying the full significance of Maori concepts such as *aroha* and *whanau*. On the other hand, he is held to fail because his fiction "tries too hard to succeed as a *pakeha* ("white") narrative . . . has no centre and nothing real happens in it." Obviously, a minority writing has to be everything at once.[1]

The major critical reservation concerning Ihimaera's work is that it is overly sentimental. While we are probably justified in finding that many of his stories tug at the heart-strings of the reader rather than dramatically presenting the emotions of a character within a compelling situation, I wonder whether Western cultural expectations do not affect our judgement when we devalue the writing because of this? Is the supposedly diffused focus of *Tangi* a failing of craft, or does it adequately express the confusion at the heart of its central figure who mourns the loss of his father? Is the "problem" in the fiction exactly the problematic differences between a *tangi* and a "funeral"? Quite apart from social conventions of how acceptable the display of emotion in public may be, does not the very concept of *aroha* suggest that sentiment may be a vital element of Maori (and possibly of pan-Pacific) literature? As Epeli Hau'ofa and Albert Wendt have demonstrated in relation to Samoa and Tonga, one result of the modern dissipation of the power of ritual and myth as a result of Colonialism and economic imperialism has been the ironic obverse to traditional valuations of love and community--the fact that sentiment shorn of its virtue is all that is left as response to life.[2] Whether we consider traditional or modern views of the culture as they are revealed in the fiction of Witi Ihimaera, it seems to me that one critic puts his finger unwittingly on a major element in post-colonial and minority literature (and perhaps especially in Maori and Pacific literature) when he says: "What seems to be at fault . . . is precisely this: that learning comes sentimentally."[3] Seen from a different angle, this fault becomes a virtue--a creative strategy for communicating with the dominant culture if not also for asserting one's particular cultural identity.

Although I am suggesting that Maori culture may place value upon modes of cognition at variance with the standards developed by a culture that has enshrined the rational intellect, I am not arguing for literary ghettos off-limits to non-members. Cultures only retain their validity through processes of interaction and revision: traditions live by being continually made modern. In fact, there is a paradox in Ihimaera's stories. Seen as "rhetorics of sentiment" they not only express a minority culture, but also partake of the heritage of European Romanticism which is New Zealand's literary birthright by virtue of British settlement and schooling. In this context, they assume, for the non-Maori critic, recognizable forms and can be seen as succeeding according to *pakeha* criteria. (Well, *selected* European criteria, since no culture is static or entirely uniform.)

Taking the traditional Maori inheritance of Ihimaera, then (the "myth and ritual" that some critics feel he is obliged to evoke), we must consider the fact that it is primarily an oral phenomenon. Western and modern "privileging" of privacy and decorum is connected with mass-communication and the need to keep everyone self-contained for fear of large-scale disruption to the running of society. Mental activity and vicarious emotional catharsis is *in*; direct expression of emotion is strictly curbed. Written prose is the order of the day. In the context of an oral tradition, direct address, communal expression, and poetic utterance may be the basis of an aesthetic. Originality and the steady refining ("deepening") of perceptions and ideas are no longer key ideals. In Maori tradition, "the purpose was . . . the forceful and ingenious statement of recognised truths."[4] The object of it all was/is the shared immediacy of response affirming collective identity and the continuity of one's place in the social, historical and cosmic order.

If we look at the Maori short-story there is a sameness about many of the examples which on first sight might indicate a lack of originality and tendency towards cliche. There is a striving for intimacy of narrative voice and a direct access to content through dramatic dialogue. Familiar situations such as a child's affection for a grandparent or an adult's realization of the loss of a child-like connection to the natural world make it easy for the unsympathetic. Given the pressures of survival in a pluralist, modern world, we can, however, see these stories not merely working out of a traditional oral context, but expressing the need to restate one's identity with new insistence in order to maintain a basis on which tradition can be brought into dialogue with white society. Insofar as many of the stories are protests against the depredations of *pakeha* colonialism they are discourses of sentiment--rage and pathos--in line with all Romantic rebellion, but they may be read in the light of the oral poetry that traditionally was defined and evaluated according to the sentiments it generated in the listener--poems of love, lullabyes, poems to curse, to shame someone for bad conduct, to maintain a sense of outrage, to mourn. Of the last type, Ihimaera says, "the emotions are worked up to a pitch at a tangi: the whole business of the ceremony is to make the people respond as one."[5] It is possible, I think, to read his stories in the context of this oral tradition and its inbuilt "sentimentality."

In another sphere of literature, the West African, Chinua Achebe, began writing novels as an exercise in anti-colonialist pedagogy. His intention was to show young Africans that life before the white man came was not "one dark night of savagery." Ihimaera's stories came about as the result of a similar idea, but they were not designed as vehicles for historical facts; rather they were intended to convey *feeling*:

> you'd think there would be something Maori to study in school, but there was nothing. The Maori language is now taught in high schools . . . but there's more in Maori culture than just the language.
>
> *Pounamu* has been reprinted several times since 1972 . . . that has delighted me, it's given Maori kids an idea of what it's like to be Maori, the emotional experience.[6]

For Achebe, whose language and culture are very much alive and a part of the modern urban world on their own terms, there can be a familiarity and confidence which allows him to treat traditional society with cool appraisal. Ihimaera, on the other hand, does not possess this kind of intimate objectivity. As a member of a "subject" culture, he has been separated from the world of tradition and as a consequence assumes a style of "academic" reconstruction and personal nostalgia. For the latter, sentiment is a natural medium of expression; for the former, it is the means of bringing the reconstruction to life:

> I was never brought up in Waituhi, the Maori village but in Gisborne. I used to stay with my grandmother in Waituhi . . . and I feel I belong there. But I was brought up at one remove. . . . I could look at the Maori way of life, take an observant point of view, and I found it marvellous. The fact that I couldn't speak the language too, put me at another remove.[7]

So it is for the alienated urban kinds such as himself that Ihimaera writes, and for them the first thing in cultural regeneration is to discover a *feeling* for *maoritanga*, since they do not yet have the learning that will bring them to an understanding of their heritage. It is only through a sentimental attachment that such learning can come about:

> I write about the landscapes of the heart, the emotional landscapes which make Maori people what they are. My first priority is to the young Maori, the ones who have suffered most with the erosion of the Maori map, the ones who are Maori by colour but have no emotional identity as Maori. My second priority is the Pakeha--he must understand his Maori heritage, must understand that cultural difference is not a bad thing and that, in spite of the difference, he can incorporate the Maori vision of life into his own personality.[8]

Both of these functions are served by the second of Ihimaera's books, the novella, *Tangi*. This is a more personal exploration that the "classroom" collection of stories, *Pounamu*, *Pounamu*,[9] but it equally reflects a social reality in that the only time that many young people return to their family village is to mourn the death of one of the older generation and to experience their separation from the traditional ways of Maori life.[10] The book is a warning as well as an instruction--it creates the emotional links to the root culture and makes clear that the whole nexus will be destroyed unless some imaginative restitution can be effected.

Tangi is potentially an exercise in sentimentality, but the author's awareness of the dangers keep the work within the bounds of an instruction in the value of sentiment. He speaks of the need to put some creative distance between his own relationship with his living father and the character Tama's strong emotional ties to his dead father, Rongo. Writing the story was nonetheless "shattering, a catharsis" through which Ihimaera "came to terms with (his) own self." The writer is clear that change is inevitable--that there has to be some blending of western and traditional Maori ways. But his discovery of selfhood through the literary rehearsal of sentimental experience of *maoritanga* realizes the need for the member of a minority culture to maintain an identity through keeping in touch with the past. As some critics have noted, there is an "ebb and flow" of intensity of feeling as well as in the movement from town to village and back within the story which embodies this dialogue between cultures.[11]

As someone with a university education who has travelled to Europe, Ihimaera is well able to exploit this dual outlook on life. Not only does he turn to Maori myths to give form to his novella and the story from which it grew, but he draws as well upon European opera. the reason in both cases is to find an artistic strategy with which to create and sustain a central emotional mood:

> The chief problem was how to sustain the sadness. My first draft was bad: it was a straight chronological story of the boy going home to his father's tangi, ending with an account of the tangi. That way there was no relief from the sadness, so I chopped the story up, going backwards and forwards in time. . . . There are lots of echoes in the book: I kept repeating myself in various ways. The repetition is in the *waiata tangi*, the funeral chants, and I use repetition deliberately: it is part of our ceremonial, and it intensifies

> the sense of grief and loss.
>
> I love opera, and got help in the imagery conveying sadness from librettos. The sense of mountains coming closer, the world closing in on Tama, comes from Catalani's *La Wally*, for instance. (The end of "The Whale" in *Pounamu*, too, when the old man sees first the gulls in the sky then the whale, has hints of "One fine day" in it.)
>
> Maori myth also helped me in the structure and in conveying grief. The Earth and Sky myth, the story of Rangitane and Papatuanuku, is mentioned in the epigraph; it's supposed to tie in with the death of the boy's father, which is as shattering an event to the boy as was the separation of Earth and Sky. Tama is mourning the loss of a figurehead, of a father protector symbolized in the legend of Rangi.[12]

Now a critic would hardly think of condemning an opera for being too lyrical or sentimental. There may be questions of how well the structure, the imagery, the rhetoric, the "atmospherics" serve to suspend disbelief and engage the audience in an emotional experience, but there can be no argument that sentiment is extraneous to the art form. Nor can the critic attach the connotations of superficiality and lack of control which go with mention of sentiment to such a consciously planned story. The critical response which demands expression of an organic, "primitive" association with tradition and nature and then takes the writer to task for being naively sentimental does not consider the choice of strategies open to a minority culture to communicate to an audience that is in these times multicultural on both sides of the ethnic division. In the case of Ihimaera's stories, if not of Maori stories as a whole, sentiment becomes the means of providing an imaginative appreciation of cultural inwardness in a style appropriate to the values of that culture.

Witi Ihimaera's stories, as in the example of "Tangi," all work towards the immediate emotional involvement of the reader at the level of feeling, but are nonetheless characterized by distancing techniques which indicate a decidedly unsentimental control of the fictional material.

In many instances, the naive world of a child narrator sets limits to the contents of the tale and gives verisimilitude to the straightforward innocence of a sentimental response to circumstances. Frequently the effect is underpinned by the conventions of an oral narrative style. This oral directness accounts for the surprising vague presence of Nanny Tama in "A Game of Cards"; it is not his story, but his wife's, so he fades into the background in order that due tribute may be paid to her memory and the dead brought momentarily to life once more. The traditional device of the framing persona of the narrator makes immediate the world of story through his obvious place within it, but distances the tale to be told inside that context. Thus Tama, at the end of "A Game of Cards," draws away from his evocation of Nanny Miro by placing her in a legendary frame, and at the same time brings himself and his story back into proximity with the world of the reader. Another example of this technique occurs in the humorous story, "The Makutu on Mrs. Jones." The reader is brought to a knowing intimacy with the ruefully reflective married man who tells the tale, and that very closeness keeps the tale itself (experienced by the man as a naive child) within ironic limits.

As this might suggest, time-frames are often important in Ihimaera's stories, and distances are also established through car trips and telephone-calls. (These usually reflect the geographical and social divide of town and country, as in "Beginning of the Tournament," "Tangi," and "In Search of the Emerald City.") Yet another controlling device which should give pause to those accusing the author of sentimentality is the organization of the stories within the collection. Richard Corballis has noted how *Pounamu, Pounamu* opens and closes with a death, and how it depicts a progressive darkening of mood as past memories merge into present realities.[13] There is also a deliberate balancing of tragedy, pathos and humour in the arrangement of the stories, just as each one can be seen as an illustration of a different aspect of the concept of *aroha* (family love, romantic love, passion, nostalgia for loved-ones long gone, neighbourly love, communal love).

Ihimaera has been accused of orchestrating a wash of colourist sentiment without linking it to the internal dynamics of character development or to a realistic grasp of the contemporary social situation. While it is true that there are moments of overwriting, and that outside of the classroom the general tone seems a little adolescent if not self-indulgent, any comparison of his stories with the rest of Maori fiction will reveal just how carefully constructed his are with regard to effectively blending character, motivation, dialogue and social setting. If the last element is restricted, it is surely Ihimaera's privilege to stick to what he knows and to leave the tougher, more political fiction to writers like Rowley Habib. It is interesting to note how his second collection, *The New Net Goes Fishing,* and the second novel, *Whanau,* deal with this contemporary urban and disaffected side of Maori life to a far greater extent.

Sentiment, especially nostalgia, may feature in the first collection of stories, but this does not lead the writer into dishonesty. There is an ever-present consciousness of change and loss to counter any facile idyllic view of the good old days, and village life is shown to be harsh and limited in scope. In "A Game of Cards," the motif of cheating sets up a countervailing image to that of the "grand old lady" and the harmoniously integrated community. Nanny Miro is fooling herself, but fooling no one, just as the narrator's grandson is aware that he is only able to "fool himself" in the temporary frame of the story's reminiscences. The facade of the old ways lasting forever is exposed, anger stands against tears, tears against laughter. As the opposites are blended into a single, caring whole, so the cheating of death through the creation of legend is opposed by the knowledge that we are all cheated by mortality. There may be sentiment, and even sentimentality in the story, but it is not unrealistic, nor as unsubtle as it initially appears.

Neither is it gratuitous or inappropriate through lack of preparatory dramatization within the story. In "Fire on Greenstone," for example, the tears Tama sheds at the end are justified because he has been led back through the halls of memory by his grandfather to take personal possession of the meaning of the tribe, the soul of the *whanau*, itself residing in the personal significance of artefacts and the recall of historical records. Had Tama come back fresh from the city to find all gone and wept while still thinking of the house as a museum, *then* we could find the story sentimental. As it is, its power rests on our learning with Tama through sentiment so that we can apprehend deeper meanings of cultural attachment that detached knowledge could convey.

"One Summer Morning" is a tale which suffers in being taken outside of the classroom. There are attempts at authorial control through the shifts from first-person to second- to third-person narration as the prose moves from dialogue to monologue to description. But adolescent self-dramatization is too 'soppy' and self-pitying to be swallowed in such a large dose and the descriptions read like sociological reportage of rather too-familiar material. Although it shows white school-children that Maoris go through the same delights and torments as they do, and it tells Maori children that their lives are valid subjects for literary treatment, it fails in itself to offer anything more seriously meaningful than a series of set domestic comedies connected by a stereotypic figure and the stock moral that growing up involves the assumption of extra responsibilities.

A story like "The Child," however, works more effectively because it has few pretensions to be other than a "mood piece" framed by memories and a child-like consciousness that precludes most of the influences of the outside world. The father's knowledge of death's inevitable approach, the antagonism of people outside the family, impinge on the caring relationship between child and senile grandmother only enough to show it as a charmed circle. Seeds of change are present within the circle, though: Nanny's decline is brought on by the death of her husband, and her grasp of Maori is faltering as the child's control of English also fluctuates (a weak point in the tale is the failure to establish a consistent voice for the child). Memory, as represented in the photos of nanny as a young woman, corresponds to the heart-warming memory that contains the whole story so that acceptance of death flows from unquestioning acceptance *aroha* to be drawn from a past that has become timeless. The concluding sentence ("Her mind had wandered far away, and my Nanny, she had wandered after it.") seems at first to be authorial cleverness punning on "wander," or one of the slightly artificial phrases used by the child (e.g., "my heart would flutter as if a small bird was trapped in there and wanted to get out.") However, the idea is consonant with traditional Maori beliefs in the duality of the self whereby the soul-self (*wairua*) can leave the body and travel during sleep, departing finally on a journey to the kingdom of the dead.[14] This correspondence enhances the feeling of continuity we find in the story and the intended idea that death can be accepted as a natural part of the rhythm of life.

A similar link to traditional mores can be found at work in "The Whale." Again, this functions as a distancing technique while it communicates possibilities of continuity with the past. Less blatantly than the language experiment in Patricia Grace's stories, Ihimaera reorders syntax and flow to hint at the Maori tongue in which the old *kaumatua's* thoughts are couched:

> He sits, the old kaumatua, in the darkness of the meeting house. All his family, they have died: parents, brothers . . . all gone. Ruia, his wife, she's been dead many years. His friends, there are none. Always he has lived here. . . .[15]

Repetition of this halting rhythm generates a slow, falling cadence that has an air of disllusion and the pace of a funeral procession. It reflects the gradual dissipation of the *aroha* and the fading of a heartbeat in both the old man and the community he symbolizes. The writing here is controlled and firm. The images of the heart neat and the hooked fish are appropriate and well sustained. The lament achieves a certain grandeur and dignity of tone which redeems it from total despair.

Once again, there is some grounding for this in Maori myth. Paikea rode a whale to Aotearoa (New Zealand). Ignoring a warning, he let it touch land, and it became an island. The island is still there to remind people of their past, and thus is a sign of both tragedy and positive maintenance of tradition. In the same way, the hooked fish represents the destruction of the whale while it also invokes the myth of Maui pulling up the islands from the chaos of an underwater world. Ihimaera therefore is able to suggest a strength underlying surface weakness, the possibility of renewal within destruction and death. Perhaps the people "hooked" by *pakeha* ways may in their weariness come to a landfall through the witness of the memories of the old people and the art of the writer who not only summons up those memories, but injects the feeling into them that will recreate the sentimental attachment to a cultural identity. Such a possibility is implied in the figure of Hera, the old man's favourite offspring. If he cannot cope with a new and ambiguous world, she may have the experience that will enable the traditions to continue. At his tangi, "Hera, his niece, she will cry very much. But in the end she will remember."

If these stories present a "rhetoric of sentiment," then they function not so much to move the reader to action in any revolutionary way. Nor are they a mawkish lament for the loss of traditional ways to a modern Western lifestyle. The stories are there to educate. They instruct us in what it is like to be Maori, how "Maorihood" is experienced, and they convey the simple but crucial message that feeling one's Maoriness is O.K. In a white settler society where roots in Romantic idealism have withered, leaving mostly a utilitarian rationality seen in the generally bleak realism of white New Zealand short-story writing), the production of "sentimental" stories is one way of defining oneself as other than *pakeha*. For the white reader, there is an education in the importance and dynamics of sentiment in Maori culture (and perhaps in what is lacking in their own). For the Maori, there is a reconstruction of those forms of sentiment which are socially significant and a reconnection through sentiment with the sources of identity. Because of this, Ihimaera's tales are not superficial; they creatively develop a communicative strategy by which a minority literature can speak to both its own ethnic group and to the world at large in terms that relate to its own culture and in forms that may be acceptable to the dominant standards of the literary machine.

NOTES

1. The description of this kind of criticism is based on Norman Simms's article, "Maori Literature in English. Prose Writers. Part two: Witi Ihimaera," *Pacific (Moana) Quarterly*, III(3), 1978. Quotations from pages 336, 338-39. The selection of the example is not intended to indicate particular defects in Simms's criticism, simply that it is typical of the dilemma under discussion.
2. Epeli Hau'ofa, *Tales of the Tikongs* (Auckland: Longman Paul, 1983); Albert Wendt, *Flying Fox in a Freedom Tree* (Auckland: Longman Paul, 1974).
3. Simms, p. 345.
4. Margaret Orbell, ed., *Contemporary Maori Writing* (Welling-

ton: Reed, 1970), Introduction, p. 1.

5. Examples of other Maori writing can be found in the collection *Into the World of Light*, ed. Witi Ihimaera and Don Long (Auckland: Heinemann, 1982). The quotation is from John Beston's interview with Ihimaera in *World Literature Written in English*, 16(1), 1977, p. 120.
6. *Ibid.*, p. 117. Achebe's statement can be found in his collection of essays, *Morning Yet on Creation Day* (London: Heinemann, 1975), p. 43.
7. Beston interview, p. 117.
8. *Ibid.*, p. 118.
9. Witi Ihimaera, *Pounamu, Pounamu* (Auckland: Heinemann, 1972); *Tangi* (Auckland: Heinemann, 1973).
10. This fact is mentioned by Keri Hulme in her article "Maori: an introduction to bicultural Poetry in New Zealand," in Harrex and Amrithanayagam, eds., *Only Connect* (Adelaide, South Australia: Centre for Research in the New Literatures in English, 1981), p. 299.
11. See Simms, p. 343, and Margaret Nightingale, "All any Man with a Club can do," in R. Sellick, ed., *Myth and Metaphor* (Adelaide: C.R.N.L.E., 1982), p. 62. A less sympathetic study of the differences between cultures is Heather Roberts's "Two Cultural Attitudes to Death," *Landfall*, 129, 1979, p. 21.
12. Beston interview, p. 119.
13. Richard Corballis, "Witi Ihimaera: Literary Diplomacy," *Landfall*, 129, 1979, p. 64.
14. Keri Hulme, "Myth, Omen, Ghost, Dream," in P. Sharad, ed., *Poetry of the Pacific Region* (Adelaide: C.R.N.L.E., 1984), p.32. Ihimaera's other works mentioned are: *Whanau* (Auckland: Heinemann, 1974), and *The New Net Goes Fishing* (Auckland: Heinemann, 1977).
15. *Pounamu, Pounamu*, p. 115.

Janet Frame: Talking Treasure

RIEMKE ENSING

Jewels feature frequently in Janet Frame's writings, but they are not the jewels we associate with material wealth and which most of us know we'll never own, the "ruby, sapphire, topaz, carnelian, fire opal, agate, moonstone, bloodstone, jasper, diamond" stones glittering on the rich. Rather they are the 'jewels' of the language which, if we are not constantly watchful, can cause confusion and even trauma.

"Words, first words, are as traumatic as first love and first death," writes Janet Frame in her ninth novel *Daughter Buffalo* relating how a young child of seven with an "almost open mind about language, prepared for any shock, and as vigilant as a soldier on sentry duty in my encounters with words," was caught unawares at school one day by the the word "jewel." The whole chapter is a hilariously comic *tour de force* recounting the anticipation, excitement, impatience and finally disbelief and disappointment when the child realizes it has been "betrayed" by a word, simply because it confused it with the similar sounding words-- "dual" and "duel." "It did not seem fair that one word could promise so much, could have held so much power to organize and disorganize my life. How could I have been at the mercy of one word? My betrayal by the word 'jewel' was a lasting blow dealt to me by the language I was encouraged to be at home in." The child, however, learns a lesson and inadvertently does receive the "jewels" it had been promised. It goes home and opens the dictionary and is "showered with the inescapable words which if I worked, could become my allies instead of my enemies."

The humour with which Frame recounts this classroom incident is nonetheless overlaid with a serious commentary on the ability of language to cause "much hope and suffering." Here, as everywhere in her work, the fact of social aloneness is emphasized and the chapter, despite its mirth and wit, ends on the observation that in "dual" desk, "imagining we sit together, we sit alone."

It is interesting to read in the autobiography incidents in "real" life which have obviously found their way back into the fiction. Or has the "fiction" become part of the "real," remembering from *Daughter Buffalo* that the child "resented the confusion felt over my inability to discern where to put a word when it was given to me, whether among the real or the unreal, especially when to me all was real."

In the first volume of the autobiography, *To the Is- land*, recounting a childhood visit to the dentist, Frame reconstructs almost the same language used by the child in *Daughter Buffalo*, except that the "betrayal" now centres round the words used by the nurse. "'Smell the pretty pink towel,' she said gently, and, unsuspecting, I leaned forward to smell, realizing too late as I felt myself going to sleep that I had been deceived. I have never forgotten that deception and my amazed disbelief that I could have been so betrayed, that the words 'Smell the pretty pink towel,' without any hint of anything fearful happening, had been used to lure me into a kind of trap."

You begin to understand why Janet Frame doesn't like to give interviews. Words have too much the ability to deceive and to be misunderstood, and as she puts it in her second novel, *Faces in the Water*, which is her "story of my experiences in [psychiatric] hospitals in New Zealand, recording faithfully every happening and the patients and the staff I had known," "conversation is the wall between ourselves and other people, too often with tired words like used and broken bottles which, catching the sunlight as they lie embedded in the wall, are mistaken for jewels."

Conversely, "Bright is the ring of words/when the right man rings them" as she learned to recite in her second year at Waitaki Girls' High School, and like the poet reaching into his own kingdom, Janet Frame has spent a lifetime "ringing the words"--"in the power of words. Driven now by a constant search and need for what was, after all, 'only a word'--imagination." Not only was the embrace of literature a solace in time of loneliness,

("I did not realize the extent of my loneliness. I clung to works of literature as a child clings to its mother") but the writing was an actual "need," an awareness that she had to write, not just to survive as an individual, although that was important after the traumatic years spent being ciphered away and "plundered" of her self-esteem as a non-person in psychiatric hospitals in New Zealand. She felt the need to "embrace the language" lest there be "constant betrayals of language." In the last volume of her autobiography she writes: "Language that had betrayed, changed, influenced, could still befriend the isolated, could help when human beings had withdrawn their help."

The "obsession" (as some critics have called it) with language is no doubt a direct result, firstly, of a childhood immersed in poetry ("Mother had turned increasingly to poetry for shelter"), song, fairy-tales ("I took Grimm's Fairy Tales to bed and began to read, and suddenly the world of the living and the world of reading became linked in a way I had not noticed before"), stories, and the practical application of words (Dad's interest in words was formal. Words were to be sought and explained.") At first, "believing from the beginning that words meant what they said" Frame gradually realized that language might not always be literal. ("I had supposed that a permanent wave meant just that, and the prospect of a word's lack of truth gave me a feeling of shock. If *permanent* was *everlasting*, like forever, like the stiffly petaled flowers in their bell jars upon the graves, then how could a permanent wave wear out?"

But perhaps even more convincingly, Janet Frame's preoccupation with *the power of words* was the fact that her writing literally saved her.

If it had not been for her first collection of stories *The Lagoon* winning the Hubert Church Award for best first book of prose while she was on the psychiatric hospital's waiting list for a leucotomy (an incision made into the frontal lobe of the brain to relieve ostensibly some forms of mental disorder, but largely unsuccessful and described by the magnificently drawn and articulate character Daphne in *Owls Do Cry*, Frame's first novel after her release from hospital), she would, in all probability, not be writing now. ("The 'leucotomies' were silent, docile; their eyes were large and dark and their faces pale, with damp skin. They were being 'retrained' to 'fit in' to the everyday world. In the whirlwind of work and the shortage of staff and the too-slow process of retraining, the leucotomies one by one became the casualties of withdrawn attention and interest; the false spring turned once again to winter." --*Faces in the Water*--her second novel, written after tests at the Maudsley Hospital in London conclusively showed that Frame had "never had schizophrenia and that she should never have been admitted to a mental hospital.")

Frame was exceptionally lucky that her doctor noticed the item announcing the literary prize in the local evening paper and that he decided to act on the detail instantly ("We're moving you out of this ward. And no leucotomy.").

As Janet Frame recounts, "it was my writing which at last came to my rescue. It is little wonder that I value writing as a way of life when it actually saved my life. . . .The winning of the prize and the attention of a new doctor . . . enabled me to be prepared for a discharge from hospital. Instead of being treated by leucotomy, I was treated as a person of some worth."

In *Faces in the Water,* the protagonist Istina Mavet is also "saved" from having a leucotomy. Not by an actual collection of published stories, but through the power of literature which an enlightened doctor empowers her to share through the services of the Country Library Mobile Van service which called at the hospital every three months and left about sixty books "of all classifications which were chosen by the chaplain or members of the office staff or perhaps the doctors or occupational therapists, but rarely by nurses or attendants who were regarded in the hierarchy as belonging to the lowest social scale." Miraculously it seems (for where would the patients count in this hierarchical scheme of things), Istina is urged out to the library van to sort books with the doctor and "the wonderful treasure" seemingly "reached only at the end of such a forbidding journey," restores her, and "from that day I felt in myself a reserve of warmth from which I could help myself, like coal from the cellar on a winter's day, if the snow came or if the frost fell in the night to black the flowers and wither the new fruit." Through the healing power of literature, she is able to leave the hospital, being told to "forget all you have ever seen, put it out of your mind completely as if it never happened, and go and live a normal life in the outside world." The final comment in *Faces in the Water* is scathing in its irony: "And by what I have written in this document you will see, won't you, that I have obeyed."

Since then, it seems, the writing, the pre-occupation with language, has been the dominant force in Frame's life and she doesn't encourage distractions. "In my struggle to get my writing done I realized the obvious fact that the only certainty about writing and trying to be a writer is that it has to be done, not dreamed of or planned and never written, or talked about, but simply written: it's a dreary awful fact that writing is like any other work."

I first "met" Janet Frame through her first two novels when, as a student during the University summer breaks in the early 1960s, I worked as a nurse-aid in that same Auckland psychiatric hospital where she had spent too many years of her life. What I experienced in that institution was horrendous and unforgettable, and Janet Frame's recreations of those unbelievable terrors, are as I myself observed and lived through them, with the very real difference that I was sometimes on the other side of the wire and could walk out. Ironically both *Faces in the Water* and *Owls Do Cry* were recommended texts for those training to become qualified psychiatric nurses. I say "ironically" because what was described in the books was daily enacted *still* on the wards, despite the mirror being held up by literature, and there was little to distinguish fact from the ostensible "fiction" of the novels. Certainly nothing much changed despite numerous later inquiries into the "treatment" (abuse would seem a more adequate word) of patients and that same hospital was recently again grabbing the attention of newspaper headlines following the controversial death of a patient.

Over the years, partly through an interest in social history--an interest in the society one lives in--(and which, interestingly, Janet Frame *wondered* about returning to when she was living in England, being advised that that might be unwise due to the intolerance of a society which constantly referred to her as "unbalanced" and "insane" since the publication of her novels), I have kept a file of newspaper clippings about the Auckland psychiatric hospital where Janet Frame spent some considerable time as a patient and out of which she wrote "the story of my experiences . . . recording faithfully every happening and the patients and the staff I had known."

Although both novels are "fiction" in the sense that Frame "borrowed" from what she had observed among patients "to build a more credibly 'mad' central character" and omitting much in order to achieve a "subdued rather than a sensational record," the society she depicts is startlingly similar to the one reported in newspaper headlines all over the country in the 1982 inquiry--some 24 years after the publication of *Owls Do Cry* which took its title from Ariel's song in Shakespeare's *The Tempest*.

> Where the bee sucks, there suck I;
> In the cowslip's bell I lie;
> There I couch when owls do cry;
> On the bat's back I do fly,
> After summer, merrily.

Oakley Nurse describes fear of ECT "torture"/Oakley nurses "laughed at sexual assault"/Ex-patient: Nurses "set on me"/ Oakley patients choked, kicked, inquiry told/Oakley conditions appal/Hospital patients stranded for years, while the *Auckland Star* editorial (11 Sept. 1982) commented: "George Bernad Shaw once said that the degree of civilization attained by any society could be measured by looking at its prisons. Winston Churchill echoed this view with his comment that the moral state of a nation could be judged by the way it treated its prisoners. We New Zealanders see ourselves as civilized, compassionate, humane. Recent disclosures about the treatment of inmates of closed institutions [prisons, secure psychiatric units, Social Welfare children's homes] suggest we may be deluding ourselves." and a columnist pleaded for "Compassion in our human zoo" consciously or unconsciously alluding to the animal imagery that makes such poignant impact in *Faces in the Water*: "the massive Matron Glass on her tiny blxkshod feet approached down the corridor, unlocked the observation dormitory and stood surveying us, with a query to the nurse, like a stockman appraising a head of cattle waiting in the saleyards to go to the slaughter-house."

The terror-invoking years between 1945 and 1954 when Frame was confined in a number of mental hospitals, is condensed to some forty pages in the autobiography. The fuller accounts can be read in *Owls Do Cry* and *Faces in the Water*, but there, as in the autobiography, it is not the graphic details, (which one gets in Jane Campion's film) but the *reflective* aspect of her prose that engages one's emotions and elicits compassion.

Although a film may capture the *physical* details of a particular landscape, (the interior of the "railway" houses for instance, is magnificently done), it cannot catch the rich allusions and analogies that are so much part of the "interior" landscape of Frame's measured and evocative prose:

> The other permanent patients lived in Ward Two. Except at E.C.T. we saw little of these people. We heard them as background noises from their special park and yard and at night when their sleeping quarters, known as the Brick Building, became like a hive with bees wailing and screaming behind the rusted wire-netting windows, as if their day's honey had been lost or never gathered. Sometimes we saw them in the evening being rushed into the Brick Building and seeming to execute a wild dance before they entered, as if to signal the direction of the flowerless fields where for one more day in the numerous years of their search they had wasted their time and yearning. And occasionally we glimpsed these same people in their dark blue smocks, their skin sun-stained and wrinkled, being driven, flanked by nurses, from the day-room of their ward to the park where they would spend the rest of the day. And then they looked sad to say, like people; we could not deny their relationship to us; but they moved, their heads bowed, their bodies half-crouching, as if they faced a driving blizzard. *(Faces in the Water)*

Frame's ability to draw one in compassionately, to go beyond the essentially graphic and enter a larger moral climate, will always give her writings the edge over any film where, particularly in scenes dealing with "bedlam" it is tempting to slip into that very "sensational" response Frame herself says she planned to subdue, "aiming more for credibility than a challenge to me by those who might disbelieve my record."

> At first Brenda played lovingly, remembering every note, although her sense of time seemed to have suffered. She

> played on and on, after a while ignoring Carol's pleas "not to play classical." Listening to her, one experienced a deep uneasiness, as of having avoided an urgent responsibility, like someone who walking at night along the banks of a stream catches a glimpse in the water a white face or a moving limb and turns quickly away refusing to help or to search for help. We all see faces in the water. We smother our memory of them, even our belief in their reality, and become calm people of the world; or we can neither forget nor help them; sometimes by a trick of circumstance or dream or a hostile neighbourhood of light we see our own face. *(Faces in the Water)*

Since returning to New Zealand in 1962, Janet Frame has lived in a number of small rural towns. Most of them (Stratford, Wanganui, Levin, Horowhenua) seem endlessly dreary--low to middle unprosperous, suburban New Zealand towns you'd expect to be conservative (frequently even "red-neck" reactionary) and heavily into rugby football. They're the kind of towns she describes in her 11th novel, *The Carpathians* for which she won both the *New Zealand Book Award* and the 1989 *Commonwealth Writer's Prize*.

> If you walk in mid-afternoon through the steets of Puamahara you might suppose you walk through a neatly kept cemetry where the graves are more spacious than usual, with flowers and vegetable gardens, fences, concrete paths leading to the door of the family mausoleum . . . and just as you become certain that you walked in a cemetry, the sounds of the living intrude and those whom you thought to be dead appear in door-ways with brooms and brushes and motormowers and hedgeclippers to perform the daily sweep and cut and snip.

As reviewer Patrick Evans has noted, Karin van Roosmalen's cover painting of the novel shows square suburban bungalows in too neat, unimaginative gardens, "their backs turned to the threatening row of distant dark mountains which evoke the jagged hills in the background of the evening town on the original cover of *Owls Do Cry*. Here too the sense is of threat imminent.

Something is going to happen."

It is difficult to understand why anyone would choose to live in the kind of towns Janet Frame seems drawn to. Possibly the reasons are financial. It's cheaper in the smaller towns. ("If I had the wherewithal I'd live somewhere else and only come here some of the time so that others could use it too). More likely, the reasons are literary. In *Living in the Maniototo* her main protagonist "did not wish to give up my home in Stratford, Taranaki, New Zealand, a small noisy town with the inevitable rose garden, clock tower, and scout den; and the streets named after Shakespearian characters. I still hope to find silence to write in this town of motor-mowing, chain-sawing, stereo-playing, panel-beating citizens. I still have faith in the town because it has a river and Shakespearian names." (In the earlier novels particularly, the references to Shakespeare are many, and the "poor naked wretches" of *King Lear* are those that populate the wards of the psychiatric institutions and Daphne as Ariel, the spirit of the imagination from *The Tempest*, is unable to find protection in a cowslip's bell. "But not any more there I couch when owls do cry. There are owls in the macrocarpa and cabbage trees and they cry quee-will, quee-will, and sometimes at night because of the trees you think it is raining for ever and there will be no more sun, only quee-will and dark."

In her autobiography, too, Frame discusses the literary aspect of returning to New Zealand: "the prospect of exploring a new country where one first saw daylight and the sun and the dark, was too tantalising to resist. . . . Living in New Zealand . . . it is possible to begin at the beginning and to know the unformed places and to help to form them, to be a mapmaker for those who will follow." *Certainly, in her often savage but accurate way she has "mapped" the New Zealand "small" towns and the sterility of the "suburbs"* "where the largest, most impressive building is not a cathedral, a community hall or theatre, but a shopping mall planned by those who believe that the commercial architecture of North America is suitable for Blenheim . . . a young new suburb named after a 'famous victory' . . . where the hammers hammer and the saws saw as the cardboard home units with their aluminium joinery, summit stone fireplaces, Wunda Kitchens, take shape in the streets of unimaginable death."

August 1984 (the year immortalized by George Orwell)

marked Janet Frame's acceptance of the *first Turnovsky Prize for Outstanding Achievement in the Arts*. Janet Frame was a schoolgirl in Oamaru, mimicking Hitler's raving speeches heard on the radio when Fred Turnovsky, (who bestows this generous annual prize in a country preferring uniformity to individual excellence) was abandoning his law studies and fleeing from Czechoslovakia to avoid the extermination camps. At the age of 23, he arrived in Wellington, physically safe but never quite escaping the problem of prejudice that had made him a refugee. In New Zealand, he and other Jewish migrants ran into attitudes which Janet Frame, eight years his junior, was then noticing at Waitaki Girls High School: "From time to time our history teacher had talked of the concept of 'purity' of 'race' which, she said , was desirable. . . . She spoke with pride of the 'purity' of the white race. Also at that time, by some subtle transmission within the community, people who were Jewish were now identified as such and often spoken of in a slighting way." Turnovsky himself, looking back fifty years in his recent (1990) autobiography recounts war-time New Zealand as more a "hostile environment" than a refuge: "Uncounted number of insults, sly or open, on trams, in the streets, in shops, in the newspapers [were] all designed to make us aware how little we were wanted." The attitude implicit here was earlier expressed by Frame in another prize-winning novel, *Living in the Maniototo* (whose title refers to an unforgettably stark, severe, and uninterrupted South Island landscape named by the indigenous Maori as "a bloody plain.") One of the characters, Zita, a foreigner, is "waiting to be chosen, approved of, by the New Zealand Government which said it was willing to 'take' some of us." She talks about New Zealand's immigration policy: "The New Zealand aim was to have people who would 'fit in' readily and painlessly (painless for those already there) like invisible mending. Or like an insect that moves to another tree and is given a new camouflage and told, stay on that bough, blend, and all will be well. Pretend you are not there. . . . Everyone said you had to be extra clever and beautiful and good and healthy to get into New Zealand, therefore most people did not try . . . it was only the quiet ones, like us, who were chosen, with all our arms and legs and cheerful smiles and clean hands and face and hair . . . we were so busy practicing to look adaptable and smiling and intelligent. . . . What a clean, healthy, people. It sounded like Paradise." Neither Janet Frame nor Turnovsky found it particularly so and as commentator Alexander Fry noted, covering the splendidly stylish occasion set in the magnificent Fowler Centre overlooking the harbour of Wellington, among ministers of the crown, chancellors of universities, judges, and the Governor General of New Zealand reading an excerpt from *Owls Do Cry*, it is interesting to reflect that here were two "outsiders" coming together to celebrate their long and respectively arduous journeys of "knocks and disappointments" through the "desert" that was New Zealand.

The need for approval usually associated with an authoritarian society intent on uniformity, exacted its terrible price from Janet Frame, but just before she began writing *Faces in the Water*, she recounted the sense of a new beginning. In *The Envoy from Mirror City*, she writes: "the 'you should' days were over. Lifelong, largely because of my own make-up, I had been a target for the *You should-ers*, with a long interval of *You must Or Else:* it was time to begin again." The change in attitude resulted in a change of name and it is a Janet *Clutha* (C.B.E.) who has a postbox at Palmerston North. It is a particularly appropriate name, taking its inspiration, one deducts from *An Angel at my Table*, from the large South Island river she had confided in as speaking for her in the context of belonging--in the same sense that Frank Sargeson's "treasured" anthology of New Zealand stories *Speaking for Ourselves* had "overwhelmed me by the fact of their belonging" although she also realized that "all writers are exiles wherever they live and their work is a lifelong journey towards the lost land."

When Janet Frame first read the New Zealand stories in Sargeson's collection, she realized that her imaginative life, which had been populated with "characters and dreams from the poetic world of *another* hemisphere," could be expressed more locally, and when she first encounters the Clutha, "a being that persisted through all the pressure of rock, stone, earth and sun, living as an element of freedom but not isolated, linked to heaven and light by the slender rainbow," she recognizes it as part of her--"I felt the river was an ally, that it would speak for me."

Like the vast-volumed, single-channelled river, pressing towards the sea through gorges and old mountain country which still, in some places, produces gold, Janet Frame has been a remarkably prolific and single-channelled producer of "treasure." Her main themes have persistently twisted, turned and surged towards finding the meaning and power of *language and the imagination* which fill a redemptive role in a frequently sterile world. Each successive volume of work is part of a continuous journey towards a further understanding of language in all its various guises and towards the tackling of an increasingly complicated writing process. Language is the jewel set in the centre of life. It is "all we have for the delicacy and truth of telling." The writer is the jeweller "who makes a long difficult journey to bring the genuine stone to one who has been deceived in his life not only by an imitation jewel but by a genuine imitation."

Nothing about the craft of writing is easy. Even self-depiction, the "life" story becomes a form of fiction, a "record with its moisture of fact and truths and memories of truths and its direction always towards the Third Place where the starting point is myth."

The process of writing fiction, the complicated and exacting business of coming to terms with the elusive and deceptive reality that is the domain of the writer, is marvellously captured in Frame's *Living in the Maniototo*--that "bloody plain" of the imagination. The protagonist is Mavis (Murness., Barwell, Halleton, perhaps in a world once peopled with Madges and Mavises and Peggy, the penultimate Mavis, yet remaining, as all good stories satisfy us by saying "to this very day," just Alice Thumb, or Ariella, Lokinia, or Maui's sister, or mere Naomi, Susan, Ngaere, Belinda. Or Violet Pansy Proudlock, ventriloquist) a writer, and woman of manifold personalities, She travels from one country to another and through the journey, explores the creative process where: "Language is the hawk suspended above eternity . . . only able by a wing movement, so to speak, a cry, a shadow, to hint at what lies beneath it on the untouched, undescribed almost unknown plain." "A house without Yeats" is unimaginable, "Words are the sole heroes and heroines of fiction" and "sentences are the smallest bedrooms. Sit, sleep, love." She has a code. It pertains to writing:

> A prose sentence which touches like a branding iron is good. A sentence which keeps its feet clean from beginning to end is good. A sentence which, travelling, looks out of

> portholes as far as horizons and beyond is good. A sentence which goes to sleep is good if the season is winter; bad, if it is early spring.
>
> A word, which is exciting to look at and say and which doesn't slop its meaning over the side, is good; a word which comes up sparkling from the well is good; a word which clusters like last year's bee around last year's flower is bad, if the flower is already dead, but good if the flower is surviving, beautiful, and alone in a place where flowers have not been known to grow and where bees never swarmed before nor gathered nectar.
>
> And so on: such is my code.

Frame too has a code. It too pertains to writing; the *serious* business of fiction which is not "putting it all down as it happens. *Writing a novel is not merely going on a shopping expedition* across the border to an unreal land: it is hours and years spent in factories, the streets, the cathedrals of the imagination, learning the unique functioning of Mirror City, its skies and space, its own planetary system, without stopping to think that one may become homeless in the world, and bankrupt, abandoned by the Envoy."

The three volumes of autobiography have been a journey of travel and imagination and metaphor. It stops about twenty years ago. The "Envoy" (the imagining self) warns her to "Take care. Your recent past surrounds you, has not yet been transformed. Do not remove yet what may be the foundation of the palace of the Mirror City. (fantasy/imagination)" The implication seems to suggest that there is "much to do"--more fiction to write before another indulgence ("I plead, 'Let me write of further travel. . . . Quick, just once"), another volume of autobiography can be written. It's time to get back to the serious business, although she confides elsewhere that she does envisage a further two volumes but won't write them until she's "almost eighty years old."

At the end of the autobiography, the "Envoy" is waiting. If we are lucky we may soon have another "treasure" from Janet Frame, who tries to keep parcelling these "gifts in language that satisfy the ear and the heart and the demands of truth."

The Lacanian Real and Janet Frame's *Living in the Maniototo*

PATRICK L. WEST

It has become a common gesture in Lacanian criticism to stress the strategic instability and looseness of Lacan's concepts and procedures. Malcolm Bowie, for one, defines Lacan as "a builder of loosely moored conceptual mobiles."[1] However, I want to suggest that while these critical moves have facilitated valuable regional and local appropriations of Lacanianism for certain political activities, they have tended--ironically--to foreclose a new and potentially fruitful understanding of *Lacanianism itself*. The position and idea of the Real stimulates this latter project not only because, in my opinion, it is a crucial key to the Lacanian text, but, more importantly, because, in the dense and weighty history of Lacanian thought, it has been misunderstood under the sign of a particular critical *uniformity* and *hegemony*. It is of great value, therefore, to my work on Frame and my work on Lacan. MacCannell's tacit definition of the Real mirrors Bowie's understanding of it as follows:

> First, the Real is that which is there, already there, and inaccessible to the subject, whether this be a physical object or a sexual trauma; when we appear on the scene as subjects certain games have already been played, certain dice thrown. Things *are*.[2]

A little later Bowie develops this interpretation with the assertion that "the Real is [also] the primordial chaos upon which language operates." (133) In short, Bowie defines the Real as a universal, ever-present stratum or foundation upon which the psychoanalytic experience constructs itself and can be constructed. It is this definition, and its unproblematic and hidden entry into MacCannell's work, that I want to counter in this paper and that serves to motivate my cultural, political and textual argument. Alan Sheridan's comment that "the 'real' is not to be confused with reality"[3] provides encouragement for my work in this respect, but it is the writing of Julia Kristeva that is particularly heuristic for this enterprise.

The sheer lack of critical work centred on the Real, combined with the peculiarly bland and homogeneous definition that has emerged, at least partially, as a result of this academic and scholarly neglect, invites and sustains the sort of analysis conducted by Kristeva in her essay "The True-Real." More specifically, Kristeva's work would seem to offer a solution to the logical dilemma apparent in MacCannell's thesis; one that manifests itself in her text as a gap between the political and cultural conditions and prerequisites of her reading of Lacan, and, the textual and rhetorical strategies that we are cued to expect will emerge from these premises. In short, MacCannell is constantly and consistently limited in respect of the material solutions and "answers" that she can develop to counter the oppressive effects of Culture. Her "literary" approach to Lacan and psychoanalysis is suggestive--and, indeed, the stress MacCannell places on *literature* serves to introduce a similar emphasis in my own thesis--but when she moves to particular literary example the limits of her theoretical paradigm become clear. An example here will serve to illustrate my point.

MacCannell's reading of Edgar Allan Poe's *The Purloined Letter* depends upon her social and cultural interpretation of Lacanian psychoanalysis. She writes:

> The Queen is *really* subject neither to the signifier as such nor to the neutral code ("the way things are") but to the specific institution of marriage in which her husband is her "Lord and Master." (33)

What MacCannell calls the *social tie* figures and supports her Lacanian analysis of Poe's short story. As far as it goes, MacCannell's interpretative work here is tenable and valid; however, in this instance, and in other places in *Figuring Lacan* where questions of "literature" are brought forward, we never get close to precisely what MacCannell claims to offer: an antidote to the hegemonic power of Culture. Her reading of *The Purloined Letter* is remarkably reductive in that, far from, in some undefined and unacknowledged way, introducing Poe's text *back into a critical engagement with Culture*, MacCannell does little more than use it to (rigidly) demonstrate the force of the *social tie*. She merely pulls back another layer of the "psychoanalytic text," and, to this extent, her reading takes on the nature and efficacy of an *allegory* of Power in its social context. Quite apart from the simple and simplifying critical and political response invited by MacCannell's naive interpretation of patriarchal, cultural power in this case, the crucial point to make is that she hamstrings Poe's text to the role of an *example*, a status constantly destined to political immobility. Despite MacCannell's protestations, we never see literature interrogating, penetrating . . . *reading* Lacan. Her own readings always mirror the rigid layout of the "psychoanalytic text."

There is, however, one redeeming feature of *Figuring Lacan* for our purposes. MacCannell's use of Lacan's *objet petit a* offers itself as a sign possibly able to resurrect her project. I will return to this at a later stage, following my discussion below of Kristeva's work on the Real.

Kristeva's difficult essay defines the True-Real by close association with "the psychotic foreclosure of the phallic signifier representing the Law of the Father."[4] Kristeva stresses the reification of the signifier, in modernist art and in the speech and writing of psychotic patients, that exposes the real for the subject. Toril Moi develops the consequences of this by arguing that

> the recurrence of the true-real or the iconic hallucination marks the confusion of the sexes, and the reduction of the other (as the site of the signifier) to a "pre-object" prefiguring the phallic signifier of the symbolic order, but situated in the Imaginary. (216)

Kristeva concludes her paper with an examination of two linguistic formations that seem to be generally intimate with the Real: demonstratives/deictics and proper names. Additionally, she introduces the concept to "literature" by reference to writers such as Antonin Artaud and Dr Schreber. Kristeva's essay is a useful and necessary rejoinder to the romanticized conception (because based on a humanist ideal of truth and reality) of the Real pushed forward by Bowie, MacCannell and others. However, it is itself accompanied by a certain theoretical anxiety that can be plotted with the help of Freud's "topographical"[5] mapping of the mind as "a system of localities arranged as strata, leading from a surface to a depth." (80) In short, Kristeva is unable/ unwilling to distinguish between the Real as identical with the semiotic *chora*, and, the Real as a pure type of linguistic indicator present only in the syntactic and phonemic *units* of language. It is clear that Moi's description of the *chora* as "a rhythmic pulsion rather than a new language . . . the heterogeneous, disruptive dimension of language, that which can never be caught up in the closure of traditional linguistic theory"[6] seems to match much of Kristeva's rhetoric in her essay; furthermore, the *chora* shares with the Real an emphasis on anality and orality. My point here, then, is that, following Freud (above), we can usefully--in the context of the colonizing, postcolonizing and postcolonized metaphors of distance and space--plot this "double-version" of Kristeva's Real as an association of *point* and *expanse*. In what follows I will explore the particular ramifications of this figuration in terms of literature and Lacan. At present, I shall be employing the Kristevean Real in its sense as a discrete function of language. I now want to turn to Janet Frame's text *The Envoy from Mirror City* because not only does it demonstrate a shifting of the "psychoanalytic text" into cultrual concern, but it provides us with a sympathetic entry into the question of literature and the Real.

In the third and final volume of Frame's autobiography, the author describes her experiences in attempting to objectively deal with and understand the nature of her "mental illness." Janet Frame's recollection of the acme of this search parallels the cultural reading of psychoanalysis that I am offering here, and, simultaneously, enables our engagement with the productive ambiguities of Kristeva's essay. There are strong correspondences between the particular positioning of Kristeva's text--that balances a medical and psychoanalytic discourse over its cultural, historical and institutional location as a seminar delivered by Julia Kristeva at the Service de psychiatrie of *Hôpital de la Cite Universitaire* in Paris--and the content and pattern of the following extract of Frame's.

> Finally I was summoned to the interview room where the medical team sat at a long table with Sir Aubrey Lewis at the head. The team had already had its meeting and formed its conclusions, and after a few minutes' conversation with me, Sir Aubrey gave the verdict. I had never suffered from schizophrenia, he said. I should never have been admitted to a mental hospital. *Any problems I now experienced were mostly a direct result of my stay in hospital.*[7] (italics mine)

Immediately following this passage, Frame compares her "diagnosis" with a prize-giving ceremony; and certainly her use of the institutional, courtroom word "verdict" cues us to the crucial shift taking place here from the schizophrenic, psychoanalytic, medical context, to one of institutions, and, more broadly, Culture. In this context, I want to make the claim that we can usefully locate the Real--in Frame's texts--in those words that emerge from and reflect Frame's cultural and social concerns: that is, to return for a moment to my introduction, in her insistent, textual listing of the artefacts of daily consumer life, the "commercial economy" of products, objects and things. To this extent, my aim is not to invigorate a particular field of cultural/social concerns through a dialectical appropriation of the strictly "medical" discourse of the Real: as Anne Maxwell seems to do, albeit with somewhat different terms, in her work on Frame, culture and Freud.[8] Rather, I want to split the idea of the Real from its accepted psychoanalytic context, and divorce it, as much as possible, from its hitherto pertaining associations. Crammed full of such textual listing, *Living in the Maniototo* provides an acute test of the possibilities of this enterprise. It is this text that I want to turn to now, bearing in mind Kristeva's heavily problematized definition of the Real, in order to pursue my study of Frame. And to frame Lacan.

The Real pushes itself forward in *Living in the Maniototo* in the frequent irruptions of "commercial language" that permeate Frame's text. The following passage will help to detail just how this process might take shape. Frame closes her description of Blenheim's houses, gardens, swimming pools, gnomes, letter-boxes (Swiss and English) and fences with this:

> --while inside the house there were the carpets named Sky Planet, Dream of the Night, Forest Splendor, Classic Plains, Mountain Glory, upon which rested the pseudo-mahogany wall-units, color TV sets, furniture with cabriole legs, turned legs, ranch-slider doors lounge suites, rocking chairs or fixed chairs with or without footstool, convertible, non-convertible. (Frame, *Maniototo*, 57)

Containning an almost hypnotic profusion of words, that affects a delimitation of our readerly and cognitive capacities, this passage, and others of its type, seem to meet the requirements of Kristeva's account of the Real. Alex Calder's paper stresses the extent to which Frame's language, in extracts like this one, is able "to elicit resistance"[9]; however, where he links this process to Frame's supposed medical schizophrenia, it seems to me, again, to be more valuable to read such resistance in terms of the properties of the Real. Not only, on one level, is it true to argue that Frame's writing above, excluding the signified and heroizing the iconic features of the signifier, engages *descriptively* with the Real, but it can be distinguished *politically* from other psychoanalytic forms. I am thinking particularly of Toril Moi's politically acute comments on the Real, taken against the blandly depoliticizing structure of "schizophrenia" which, while it enjoys a certain currency in cntemporary cultural discourse, lacks the political efficacy of the Real because it does little more than reify the "desiring flow" of language.[10] The general point should be clear. I have chosen to privilege the category of the Real because the direct concerns of *Living in the Maniototo* invite the introduction of a term politically worthy of their rhetoric. And it is the direct concerns of Frame's text that I want to turn to now.

An initial strategy here might be to place Frame's text in the postcolonial matrix dictated by her New Zealandness. To this extent, it seems useful to link *Living in the Maniototo* in a series with *The Carpathians*. *The Carpathians* was published almost a decade after *Living in the Maniototo*, and it seems to incorporate into its own textuality the historical and cultural changes that have marked Maori/ Pakeha relations in recent New Zealand history. In addition to this, Frame's later text arrives as a more sophisticated negotiation of the literary, linguistic and cultural/ historical issues first raised in *Living in the Maniototo*. The differences between the two texts can therefore be read along the lines of this fundamental similarity. Linked closely to this post-colonial reading of Frame's work is her own emphasis on the artefacts of modern consumer life. Indeed, while the bulk of critical information on Frame appreciates the importance of language in her texts, most critics fail to engage with the intimate relationship she develops between language and the *objects* of consumerism. In those locations in *Living in the Maniototo* where the Real emerges--where the linguistic sign stands only for it-self--we move away from the "playfulness" supposedly typical of Frame's writing and into virtual cataloguing of products, brands and objects. The one comes to be the other. The question that emerges here is how to read these specific and particular sites in terms of *Living in the Maniototo* taken generally?

The difficulty that emerges in any attempt to read the dis-crete functions of the Real in terms of the remainder of Frame's text is attendant upon the particular shape and structure of *Living in the Maniototo*. Kristeva's paper, in Moi's words, argues that "the true-real falls outside the framework of what is considered intelligible or plausible in the socialized space of the symbolic order." (216) This formulation implies that the Real is constantly "breaking-away" from steady and present field of the Symbolic: a space, in other words, that manifests itself most obviously in the narratorial and authorial/authority devices of the realist novel. The problem we come across with *Living in the Maniototo* lies in equating this definition of the Real and its activity with the subversive and constant anti-realism of Frame's text. *Living in the Maniototo* gainsays any possible realist interpretation to the extent that, as Patrick Evans comments, "there is no larger narrative carrying the novel's meaning."[11] Furthermore, it achieves this negation or foreclosure of realism without, in my opinion, any necessary or contingent reference to the generic forms of so-called "postmodern" literature. In other words, I want to remove my reading of Frame's work from any easy association with the broad categories of Postmodern culture, or, the various theoretical and political positions that have devolved their logic upon "postmodern" concerns. The point here is that we cannot confidently "ricochet" these Real instances in Frame off a steady, Symbolic basis in her text; nor, however, can we gather our critical interpretation around any possible politics of the Postmodern. The very title *Living the Maniototo*--which refers to a geographical feature of New Zealand--directs our attention to a specific and concrete analysis of New Zealand's cultural position and context.

This brings me to the central gesture of my interpretation of *Living in the Maniototo*. Frame's text, I want to suggest, effectively attempts to "write the Real" in the precise terms of New Zealand's postcolonial placement. Its textual concerns, organized around those discrete Real elements of the text that I have been "picking on" to date, therefore provide a basis for the future strategies of this thesis. To this extent, we are cued to the value of a critical reading that, while retaining questions of "language" and "What it is like to be a writer," (Evans, 381) highlights the commercial/consumer pressures operating on culture. I have found parallels to this sort of interpretation in Carol MacLennan's article "Dichotomous Values in the Novels of Janet Frame." MacLennan argues, in brief, that Frame's novels deconstruct the structures of power by which language is constrained to support various ideological positions and praxises. Her study usefully pushes a *cultural* reading of Frame's work, but it falls down to the extent that it relies upon a "close-fit" of signifier, signified and referent--a theoretical assumption that is inadequate to the complex demands of New Zealand's cultural relationship with and to consumerism. It is in this context that the activity of linking Frame's writing with the processes of deconstruction proves valuable. *Living in the Maniototo* acts to replicate, in language, the "signifier-exclusive" linguistic effects distributed through the sheer multiplicity and heterogeneity of everyday *objects* of consumerism. The text seizes upon the specificity of the consumer product because it allows a genuine engagement with the "fact" of postcolonialism (an entity supported by the logic of a "signifier-exclusive" economy), *and also,* through an emphasis on the physical existence, the "thingness," of the consumer object, the possibility of an exploration of the specific regional consequences of New Zealand's colonial history. In a moment I will explore Frame's links with deconstruction; for now, I want to stress the content of her position here. Frame's work aligns itself with the "commercial economy" of products, objects and things, but it avoids the potential political disability of such a "worldwide," "schizophrenic" approach by concentrating in addition on the particularity of the consumer object, and thus, by immediate extension, on the local concerns of New Zealand itself. This position engages with Anne Maxwell's comments on the problematic notion of "cultural identity," comments that implicitly highlight the necessity of a New Zealand culture sensitive to (putatively) indigenous concerns and the colonial influence. (179-80) I want to move now to some examples of how this might work in *Living in the Maniototo*; however, I again want to stress just how much this text is an experimental forerunner to the strategies Frame expounds in *The Carpathians*.

To the extent that Frame's text seeks to inhabit the iconic structure of language found in the lists of consumer products that it pushes forward, it can be linked with the processes of deconstruction. However, *Living in the Maniototo* inhabits, not in order to release a semiotic flow of traces of *différance*--the "schizophrenic" policy--but so as to constrain and contain language and language-production. This proposal clashes with the bulk of critical activity on Frame that centres on the apparent "joy" she takes in language. I want to counter this by arguing that--like Lacan?--Frame's textual and cultural politics are not identical with the manifest activity of her writing. In fact, *Living in the Maniototo* rejects any confidence we might have in a postcolonial politics based on linguistic play or desire: it precisely links such notions of language to the concerns of colonial power over New Zealand culture. To this extent, it should be apparent that the Real, in this thesis, is not simply a preliminary theoretical "idea," but that it is continually intimate with the strains and pressures of Frame's texts. I refer to two examples. Lewis, the first husband of the multi-named narrator/character, suffers a stroke and becomes "ill" with excessive fits of language. The stroke "had taken away his judgment, had levelled his tongue to all talk, and left him with a difficulty in naming, with the result that he used definitions in place of nouns." (26) Frame sharpens her political intention here, using a motif heavily imbued with postcolonial significances, in a passage that relates the trouble Lewis has in conveying the radio-message that Blenheim (in New Zealand) will be getting a twin city, Berkeley, in the USA. I want to argue that Frame uses this episode to point to the position of

New Zealand as a cultural victim/casualty of the "language-wild" USA. However, even in *Living in the Maniototo*, Frame does more than simply position New Zealand as a postcolonial victim, she also starts to initiate defensive strategies for New Zealand culture to adopt. With what I sense as a certain disgust or nausea at the endless play of language, Frame writes:

> The women's magazines printed regularly long serious articles with such titles as, "Dare I Wash My Woolen Blankets?" and "The Risk of Washing Woolen Blankets," sometimes pages of "Hints on Washing Woolen Blankets." (228)

She follows this passage with a gradual "paring-down" of language to the point where one word--*Kaiapoi*--comes to stand for wool.[12] It is worth quoting at length:

> It seemed that, among all the products of the earth, wool was the most important, especially when our early education dealt largely with products, with the implication that living depended less upon the heartbeat and import and export of breath than upon the import and export of products: wool, butter, mutton. In recent years there was even a prime minister who came from the home of blankets--*Kaiapoi*, and brought, naturally, a new share of warmth and compassion to the nation. How could he help it, coming from *Kaiapoi*? (229)

Her shifted emphasis to the product wool (as opposed to the consumer product: Woolen Blankets), aligned with her use of the word *Kaiapoi* as a locus of the Real, serves not only to introduce the concerns made explicit in *The Carpathians*, but, to begin a radical process of language that seems to conclude, in some senses, her project, and, indeed, my thesis. As I will argue at a later stage, Frame's strategy of "paring-down" language does not end in a moment of absolute erasure, but, moving through this moment, Frame ultimately develops a new and frightening language located, one could say, on the "reverse of language." However, I now want to spend some time on the other side of my project: the attempt to *frame* Lacan.

Living in the Maniototo localizes and disrupts the procedures of Lacanian theory as much as any literary text counters theoretical structures with its own regional concerns. I want to highlight this process in Frame's text in order to open-up the space introduced by MacCannell where "literature" takes a form radically capable of *reading* and infiltrating Lacanian thought. Frame's work thus becomes a site receptive to our attempt to frame Lacan in a way that transcends the limitations of MacCannell's own perspective on the interplay of text and theory; in particular, we can hope to go beyond her controlling and allegorical reading of works such as *The Purloined Letter*. The consequences of this project can be theorized dialectically with Lacan reading literature, literature Lacan, and so on backwards and forwards in continual oscillation: the categories of theory and text constantly inhabiting one another. This problematizes the filiation of Lacanian theory, and indeed, in this perspective, of modern fiction itself; however, while I want to claim a certain general utility for my comments here, I don't want to fail to stress that it is New Zealand that occupies the central position of importance in my work.

Living in the Maniototo arranges and organizes its general textuality around those common textual instances in which consumer products and objects are listed to excessive length. I have been reading these passages in terms of the Real. From this we can make two points. First of all, we are led to the general observation that our application of theoretical, (Lacanian) paradigms to Frame's text seems necessarily to invite, via the logic of reciprocality, the reverse operation: a movement of the text towards Lacanianism. And secondly, *Living in the Maniototo* stands particularly susceptible to this move because of the comfortable reception that it affords the theoretical concept of the Real: the inordinate length to which Frame's listings expand seems almost, at times, to occlude, or place under a penumbra, the activity of her other textual devices.

While all of Lacan's key concepts occupy a peculiarly shifting status, two--the *objet petit a* and the Real--stand apart for their complete remoteness from any form of definition or translation. The Real stands out to the extent that the word lacks, (except in a potentially huge, and by that measure hopeless, way,) the descriptive qualities present in the Symbolic and the Imaginary (concerned respectively with symbols and images). The *objet petit a* is left so blatantly untranslated by Lacan that Sheridan accords it "the status of an algebraic sign" (xi) and MacCannell notes its "suggestion of abjection." (167) On the particular level of Lacan's writings, therefore, each term(?) has or is a certain vacancy--a surface clear for the inscription of meaning or meanings. Furthermore, Kristeva's ambiguous definition of the Real as clustered about the concepts of point and expanse engages with a similar tendency in MacCannell's account of the *objet petit a:* Lacan's demand that this latter concept be viewed both metaphorically and metonymically can be taken, spatially, as a hint that the *objet petit a* can be pictured as an *expanse* (the "new totality" of the metaphor) and as a *point* (the "restricted domain" of the metonym). Now, the first point to make from all this is that not only do we maintain a potentially valuable homology between the postcolonial concerns of *Living in the Maniototo* and the postcolonial associations of *point* and *expanse* directed through the concepts of the Real and the *objet petit a* (New Zealand/The World), but this strategy stands as a desired/enabling sign of just how radically the literary text can actively infiltrate structures of (Lacanian) theory. The second point to make is that the Real and the *objet petit a* linked in a matrix of identity, can now be read as the space of/for literature at the very heart of Lacanianism. As "two-making-one," the Real and the *objet petit a* can be understood as orbiting inside the domain of Lacanian thought. In a complex tension, shot through with factors of attraction and repulsion derived, on the one hand, from their notional congruity and, on the other, from the disjunction rooted in their variant appellations, the Real and the *objet petit a* bounce atoms from one to the other of their respective blank surfaces. The reader, the text; the writer, the text; the page, the word . . . the "logic of two" common to all forms of literature allows me to make the claim that these two strangely orbiting bodies *attract to themselves/itself* the space and the body of literature. A concrete example drawn from Lacan's *Ecrits* will help us understand more fully the nature of this *objet petit* (Re) *a* (1).

In the essay "The agency of the letter in the unconscious or reason since Freud" Lacan follows his famous appraisal of Saussure's formula S with a short account of the difficult symbolic effects consequent upon the arrival at a station of two train-passengers, brother and sister, with an eye to the signs passing by outside. This example, however, quickly gives way to the following paragraph:

> But enough. It is beginning to sound like the history of France. Which it is more human, as it ought to be, to evoke here than that of England, destined to tumble from the Large to the Small End of Dean Swift's egg.[13]

What are we to make of what appears, at first glance, to be little more than nonsense? To take the final clause first, it seems to me significant that Lacan *collapses* the cultural position of the author, (that is, Dean, not Jonathan, Swift), with his textual and literary construction of the Lilliputian/Blefuscudian egg-controversy. What Lacan is trying to work through here is a cultural and literary reading of his psychoanalytic theory/text. To get an idea of just how thorough and radical a process this might be we have to turn to Lacan's comments on the case of Dora. Lacan reads Freud's highly self-conscious and defensive claim "'pour faire une omelette it faut casser des oeufs' (you have to break eggs to make an omelette)"[14] by playing on the similarity of "omelette" with "hommelette"/male child. Gallop defines the point more clearly: "One could, following that lead, read the proverb as meaning "you have to break eggs [penetrate and fertilize oval] to make a little man [a baby].'" (156 n4) Now, what I have just done artificially for argumentative clarity, occurs naturally, I want to stress, throughout Lacanianism as a result of the mass and massing of literary/cultural "moments" in Lacan's writings. (And, to continue this chain of thought a little longer, the effect I have just noted is potentially intensified in the increasing bulk of "Lacanian discourse" that continues to appear even since Lacan's death). The general point should, however, be clear: between these two positions/writings lies the always-already-present shift in Lacanian praxis from a medical and scientific context to a literary and cultural context. So, let me add the suggestion, in reference to the paragraph quoted earlier, that Lacan's relationship to French history may just be closer to the politics of Frame's relationship with New Zealand than may have been thought possible. Also in this context, it should be noted that I am aligning my thinking here, for the moment, with MacCannell's observation that "Under pressure from Lacan's concepts, literary criticism, the reading of literature, *becomes* a culture criticism," (129) I want to read the consequences of the above back into the concepts of the Real and the *objet petit a:* the *objet petit* (Re) *a* (1).

It seems to me that the terms Real and *objet petit a* are filled, in Lacan's work, by the excessive cultural and literary references that inhabit Lacan's writing; in particular, the *Ecrits*. It should also be plain that it is here too that I see other bodies of literature making a radical entry into the multiplicity of the Lacanian text, and, still further, into the *objet petit* (Re) *a* (1). This suggestion points clearly to the true limits of Lacan's project because it delineates the insufficiency of a Lacanian reading based only on the "theoretical" and "structural" components of his work. The example from Swift can, *at a pinch*, be read as a strict copy of the Lacanian impulse from Imaginary to Symbolic: breaking the larger end, "the primitive way of breaking eggs before we eat them,"[14] can be viewed as an Imaginary presentation of a social activity defined largely by virtue of its being anterior to the irruption of the Symbolic (Law) . . . "Whereupon the Emperor his father published an edict, commanding all his subjects, upon great penalties, to break the smaller end of their eggs." (85) Now, while this can, perhaps, be encapsulated in its context as a disparaging slur cast by Lacan on England's culture, I want to argue that all our readerly and cognitive senses rebel against the patent inadequacy of such a 'thin truth.' We bring to this passage (in Lacan) our igrained knowledge of Jonathan Swift, Dean Swift and the canonical text *Gulliver's Travels*. Motivated by the gesture that highlights the fact that, in English translation, the *a*, in *objet petit a*/ *objet petit* (Re) *a* (1) can stand, not for O/other (Autre/autre), but for *a*, the first letter of the alphabet, the primary unit of all written and spoken literature, we can radicalize MacCannell's propositions.

NOTES

1. Malcolm Bowie, "Jacques Lacan," *Structuralism and Since:*

From Levi-Strauss to Derrida, ed. John Sturrock (Oxford: Oxford UP, 1979), p. 122.
2. Juliet Flower MacCannell, *Figuring Lacan: Criticism and the Cultural Unconscious* (Critics of the Twentieth Century; Lincoln: U of Nebraska P, 1986), p. 133.
3. Alan Sheridan, "Translator's Note," *Ecrits: A Selection*, by Jacques Lacan, trans. Alan Sheridan (London: Tavistock, 1977), p. x.
4. Toril Moi, Introduction, "Le vreel," by Julia Kristeva, in *Folle verite: verite et vraisemblance du texte psychotique*, ed. Julia Kristeva and Jean-Michel Ribette (Paris: Seuil, 1979), pp. 11-35. Rpt. as "The True-Real," *The Kristeva Reader*, by Kristeva, ed. Toril Moi, trans. Sean Hand (Oxford: Blackwell, 1986), p. 216.
5. Bice Benvenuto and Roger Kennedy, *The Works of Jacques Lacan: An Introduction* (London: FAB, 1986), p. 80.
6. Toril Moi, *Sexual/Textual Politics: Feminist Literary Theory* (New Accents; London: Routledge, 1985), p. 162.
7. Janet Frame, *The Envoy from Mirror City: Autobiography 3* (1985; London: Paladin/Grafton-Collins, 1987), pp. 115-16.
8. E.A. Maxwell, "Postcolonial Intellectuals: The Politics of Cultural Criticism" (Diss., Univ. of Melbourne, 1990), p. 193.
9. Alex Calder, "The Closure of Sense: *Janet Frame, Language, and the Body*," *Antic,* 3 (1987), p. 94.
10. I have in mind here Fredric Jameson's "Postmodernism, or The Cultural Logic of Late Capitalism." My major criticism of Jameson's paper is that his definition of the "postmodern" scene as "schizophrenic" enables a *totalizing* perspective on contemporary culture that forecloses the possibility of any marginal or "resistant" politics. In short, I want to work against the universalizing tendency of Jameson's work to collapse all cultural activity (including, by implication, colonizing forces) to the "omnipotence of the Signifier."
11. Patrick Evans, "Janet Frame and the Art of Life," *Meanjin,* 44, 3 (1985), p. 381.
12. I want to place my interpretation here in opposition to Maxwell's. Maxwell writes: "At several places in her narrative Mavis refers to a woman's language which excludes men; for example, wives' gossip, and magazine articles on the mysteries of washing woollen blankets. *All carry positive*

associations and mark the 'eccentric' space of women." (187, Italics mine) As my comments in the text indicated, I think Frame places very much a *negative* pall on these magazine articles. Furthermore, it is the contrast I see between this negativity/disgust, and the following "*Kaiapoi*" paragraph, that allows me to read the latter passage positively and against its mildly ironic tone. For other examples of what I see as Frame's disgust at the endlessness of language see 25, 26, 36, 47, 51-52, 90, 109, 113, 148-49, 168, 192, 223 and *passim*.

13. Jacques Lacan, *Ecrits: A Selection,* p. 152.
14. Jane Gallop, *Feminism and Psychoanalysis: The Daughter's Seduction* (Language, Discourse, Society; London: Macmillan, 1982), p. 156 n4.
15. Jonathan Swift, *Gulliver's Travels,* ed. Peter Dixon and John Chalker (Penguin Eng. Lib., 1726; Harmondsworth: Penguin, 1967, p. 84.

The Memory Flower, the Gravity Star, and the Real World: Janet Frame's *The Carpathians*

ALISON LAMBERT

Any discussion of Frame's work needs to take into account her ongoing preoccupation with the marginalized. In *The Carpathians* (1989),[1] several new characters, representing facets of construction of New Zealand identity, join the family of the aged, the insane, the artists, and other social misfits that Frame has brought in out of the cold. I have not made especial reference to existing criticism on Frame, since this is accessible, or may be relatively familiar to readers. Nonetheless, as a sympathetic reader of Frame, I have found, through an examination of the novel's point of view, structure and imagery, an implied authorial ideology that strongly critiques present societal values (where money and progress are all-important) and hints at an alternative based on non-materialistic modes of perception.

New Zealand was recently described in the media as being:

> a tiny nation at the posterior of the Pacific with a comparative advantage in trees, grass, and--until [a recent defeat]--rugby union.[2]

The article, written by an economics editor, is titled "What's Really Wrong with New Zealand and Why Australia is Different," and stresses the problems New Zealand faces in being a society "in transition . . . driven by economic forces [it] cannot deny . . . at once irrevocably committed to change and deeply resentful of it." Rather than examining the nature of the "economic forces," Wood emphasizes New Zealand's struggle to accommodate them, thereby subtly apportioning blame.

The following extract from a New Zealand journal gives an example of this ethos at work, where re-afforestation is lauded after "most [of the native timber] was felled and burnt in the process of clearing forest to make way for farming." Replanting, however, consisted mainly of the imported Radiata pine:

> the choice could scarcely have been better: it was easily propagated and easily planted; it grew rapidly from the time of planting; it produced a large volume of wood in a short time; its rapid growth readily smothered competing vegetation.[3]

These two articles show the layers of colonization at work, and colonizing powers's assumption that the country is a "small, young land." (60) In colonizing, such terminology means to be without identity, ready for imprinting, guidance and exploitation by the "real," dominant culture, in this case the original European one borrowing from and intersecting with the acme of capitalism--the United States. The point of view of the colonized is not considered relevant; they are to be hushed, like children, until they are "mature" enough to take on the ideas of their parent-colonizers.

Hélène Cixous's work on binary oppositions[4] demonstrates how Western patriarchal thinking sites power on the side of the masculine, white, rational culture, and how such thinking is death-dealing to the feminine, to nature, to blacks and, by extension, to cultures different from the dominant one. But the dominant culture, the "centre," is invisible in that it assumes its own normality without seeing the need to name the parameters of its own ideology:

> In our society dominant discourse never tries to speak its own name. Its authority is based on absence . . . [not only] of the various groups classified as "other" . . . [but] of the specificity of the dominant culture, which is simply assumed to be the all-encompassing norm.[5]

The Carpathians subverts the binary thinking outlined above, as it is commonly applied to New Zealand, in the dominant ideology. With the exception of Mattina, the main character, who is somewhat of a paradox in that she is a wealthy New Yorker who must go outside her own culture to find and give meaning to her life, characters reflect either one side or the other of the standard binary assumptions. Those who most overtly represent the dominant economic culture, the business men, are counterposed with those usually marginalized, the old, the insane, the feminine; the latter are valorized, the former, demoted, via imagery, irony, paradox and narratorial manipulation of point of view.

According to feminist theory, it is the (masculine) job of culture to control the (feminine) unpredictability of nature: hence science, industry, technology--and the overthrow of cultures which co-exist with nature and have done so for far longer than the present dominant regime of exploiting and destroying natural resources. Frame uses two devices to signify human dependence on nature and the need to overthrow the human construction of duality: these are, respectively, the Memory Flower, and the Gravity Star. It is the legend of the Memory Flower which draws Mattina to New Zealand; the legend which describes how the "young woman, chosen by the gods as collector of the memory of her land . . . tasted the yesterday within the tomorrow." (11) The Gravity Star, which abolishes concepts of duality such as near and far, is activated in Puamahara in Kowhai Street where Mattina is staying, with the eventual effect that the residents lose their language and stand about "transformed to a . . . state of unbeing and unknowing" (129)--a state where potentially a new mode of understanding may arise:

> No town could be immune to the planting of new myths and legends, for were not these the few ways in which human beings may live, without disaster, in both the known and unknown world? (130)

Myths and legends generally come from a past so distant that no one knows who first told them; they represent a continuity of culture, whereas individuals are transient. Western civilization has largely thrown out its myths; in this rational age they would doubtless be placed on the feminine, irrational side of the binaries. Teresa L. Ebert discussing Bazin's study of Virginia Woolf's ideas on androgyny, describes the "female" mode of perception as "that design or web connecting the diversity of reality into a permanent whole."[6] 'Ebert outlines the opposing binary male and female modes of understanding: the former, "knowing in terms of apartness," with emphasis on the temporal and the inevitable outcome of death; the latter, "knowing in terms of togetherness," "the mystical, spiritual unity beyond the particular." While Woolf felt it was important to experience a balancing and interweaving of the two modes (Ebert, 152), Frame's method of dealing with duality is more like setting a couple of acrobats on a seesaw: one is up, then the other, then they change sides almost too quickly to see; the Gravity Star centres over the seesaw which suddenly spins round in a circle instead of going up, down, up . . . spinning so fast there is only a still blur of colour, a "mystical, spiritual unity."

Where then, or what, are the Carpathians?

> The Carpathians are a great mountain system, extending from Bratislavia to Orsovo, in crescent form . . . the region is wild and fertile and well-wooded with oaks, beeches, evergreens, firs, and wild animals are found, including the wolf, bear and lynx, the chamois and ibex; the bearded vulture is found there. (66)

--a remote and unheard-of location indeed, unless you happen to live there. New Zealand, where much of this book is set, is also considered to be a long way from "anywhere," often even by those who live there; "anywhere" in this place being New York. Thus are established the opposites of place; however, the associated inferior/superior dichotomy, the "us/them" way of thinking, is overturned in the course of this novel.

Puamahara is a town set in the Maharawhenua, in the lower North Island of New Zealand, and claims fame via its recently rediscovered "Memory Flower" legend of the Maoris. This attracts Mattina, who likes to use her money travelling to "out-of-the-way" places getting to know the people. Kowhai Street, where Mattina stays for two months, serves metonymically for all strange places, as what is normal to the residents there, is new to Mattina.

The name "Puamahara" is obviously of Maori origin. *The Dictionary of Maori Place Names*[7] gives the following meanings: *Puaha* means "mouth of a river"; *Maharahara*, "to keep in remembrance another's fault"; *Whenua*, "land" or "country." "Maharawhenua" therefore can be loosely translated as the land which remembers another's fault; "Puamahara" could be the source or heart of that memory. The Memory Flower, then, refers to more than the peaceful-sounding "Memory Land" (11); the area's fertility is fed by "the bones of vanished rivers and the blood of former generations." (12)

However, Tyne Street, Puamahara's main street, is a picture of present-day commerce and industry. It is:

> busy, noisy, with cars and large trucks laden with a variety of goods--glossy new cars strung like an open necklace along the length of the trucks and glittering in their sun-struck gaudy colours; sheep crowded in double layers, their glazed eyes staring through the slats as they trampled, turned and jostled, bleating and stinking, their excrement draining through a pipe outlet that emptied its foul trail into the street while pedestrians hopped and leapt aside to avoid the splashing (46)

--no tourist brochure offering, this. The trucks are loaded with "goods"; Puamaharians repeat their certainty of United States's superiority in respect to the goods "like a cultural doffing of the cap to the Master." (47) Modern civilization increasingly thinks it must have its commodities; the U.S. does not have the monopoly of this consumer ethos, though it is often seen as the innovator in inventing yet more and more consumer items. An extended metaphor throughout the novel shows this material wealth to be a bigger and better barrier to reality; a giant collective blanket keeping out the cold. As with most shared blankets, though, some get more than their fair share.

There is paradox and irony in the way Frame presents the commodities, the goods. The cars and the sheep on the trucks appear, at first, as respectively "good" and "bad"; the cars are described in terms of celebration, the sheep of degradation. But in the Shannon's house, where Mattina is invited to dinner, the "white polished goods" including the "beheaded white-bodied refrigerator" are "shining to attention," giving Mattina an undefined sense of unease with their "gloss and polish." (58) These mass-produced objects are reminiscent of soldiers; well trained, their individuality indoctrinated out of them [beheaded], seemingly ready to serve, but in fact ready to serve only the interest of the dominant class, those who can afford them. All that glitters is not gold. . . . The Shannons are serving "good old lamb" (58); a traditional standby in defiance of the experts, usually from overseas, who are "always trying to make [New Zealanders] eat some other food"--or trying to make them accept ideas other than their own.

Ed Shannon, who runs a computer shop, wants to know more about Silicon Valley; a place name metaphoric of modern industry and technology. Death is suggested too, by the modern disease silicosis, and by the valley (of the shadow of death). The negative effects of industrialism are thus linked with the U.S., yet Ed (dead?) wants to know more about it. He is a computer buff at home as well as at work, to the extent that he has dark circles under his eyes. (58) This is a New Zealander who does not go into the mountains at weekends as Mattina assumes, where he might become spiritually recharged, but who has instead become "fair game" (58) for the imported capitalist machine.

There is further death imagery in the section describing Mattina's dinner with the Shannons, reinforcing the idea that the influence of capitalism has a negative effect on New Zealand, helping kill its own identity--the individuality that Mattina has come especially to see. Renée Shannon sees Puamahara's Memory Flower legend as having been "done . . . to death" (overcooked?) by the Tourist Corporation (the body); she wonders that Mattina really did come to New Zealand for the sake of the legend. (60) Renée's cynicism effectively negates the importance of the legend, which Mattina likens to a computer programme that determines the past, present and future; "you could say that here in this fertile district, your past, your present and your future have been programmed." (60) The passage can also be read to mean that the past is the fertile district, now "discovered and recorded," and programmed in the language of the colonizers.

Renée and Ed Shannon have fallen for the consumer-based way of life. Ed is ambitious, "eager to seize an opportunity that would let him and his family penetrate deeper the suburban glories offered with future higher salary and status" (53); while

Renée thinks Puamahara is "nothing but a dump . . . a home for geriatrics" (54) and longs for busy, noisy Auckland. Renée's views emphasize her sense of marginalization, and that of New Zealand. A common remark made proudly, is that "Auckland is getting to be like New York!" (47)--New Zealand is catching up with the leader. But Mattina, paradoxically, sees Puamahara as "the centre." (60) Similarly, many important characters in this book are old, recently dead, autistic, or simply self-marginalized by feeling like "strangers" in the town they may have lived in for twenty years.

This family offers Mattina only a meal when she visits. When Mattina tries to initiate discussion of the meaning of the Memory Flower, the legend that is the reason for her visit to Puamahara, the parents either cannot or will not engage with her at this level:

> "Little old Puamahara!" Ed said, slightly mocking.
> "Just fancy," Renée said.
> "It's too up-in-the-air for me," Ed said. (61)

There is a repetition of "saids" from Ed and Renée, echoing their banal rhetoric of the diet of elsewhere. It is their child Peter who corrects Mattina's statement that this country is small and young, saying; "We are old . . . old as old." (60) Peter also sees clearly, in the way of the young, the reality of the recent murder in Kowhai Street; he "spoke obstinately," connecting the real murder with the murder games his father likes to play on the computer. (61-62) Peter is silenced by the adults; his mother reprimands him, and Mattina changes the subject. Youth and new ideas are not to be taken seriously. This is only a child, as New Zealand is a "small young land." Peter's vision, that might have fed the "lambs" as the Biblical Peter was asked to feed Christ's lambs (John 21: 15), is sacrificed.

Peter's male parent, Ed, represents business and commerce, with his computer shop. Ed plays murder games on his computer which, as Peter points out, he takes very seriously, though he denies such strong involvement. But the stick figures on his computer games "dart . . . to and fro on the screen dodging bullets," or when waiting to be shot at, dance "up and down letting out a cry with each leap, 'Help, help, help!'" (46) In a series of seemingly unconnected motifs, Ed is revealed as an enemy agent, one who has sold out, sold his soul. Silicon Valley, the American symbol of the industrial ethos, is also a symbol of death. Ed wants to spread this foreign virus throughout his country and be an area manager. (54) The stick figures that are the computer's object have no choice but to be shot at. They dance up and down, calling for help, but who is to take mere stick figures seriously? Frame's characters have been calling for help ever since her first novel *Owls Do Cry,*[8] where Daphne, incarcerated in the mental home, returns the letter from her "normal" sister Chicks having added "help help help" at the end. (101) Does Chicks know that she herself needs help, and anyway, who, or what, is going to help?

On the Shannon's computer games, there are;

> creatures with different weapons, speech-weapons, scent-weapons, listen-weapons, where a sentence in their alien talk was their army, a song their weapon, their thoughts like laser beams. Peter could destroy them, though, with earth-weapons, for that was how the game was programmed. It was obvious that Peter enjoyed being in Space. (56)

Ed Shannon thinks his son Peter is a "funny kind," a "dreamer," who "could never get facts right." (56) Yet Peter can stay "airborne for hours in Reality Mode" shooting down the enemy. Peter's qualities, coupled with the returning significance of his name and his appreciation of the legends and age of his country, (60) place him in the feminine mode of sensitivity to values which are non-materialistic and non-rational. His "earth-weapons" can be related to nature, past technologies, and therefore with the qualities valorized on the Maori marae which Mattina visits with Hene. (82-88) Far from being useless, Peter demonstrates the tendencies admirably suited to citizenship in "the human country." (51) In contrast, the "space-weapons" connect with the alien future and present, under siege by the consumer way of life with its over-riding noise of advertising of which people say "you've got to have it," wagging their heads wisely, "that's the real world." The only ones who've "got to have it" are those few who stand to make money from this rape of minds (and resources); the hard-headed business moguls of the (masculine) "active, busy world of daily activities, scientific accomplishment, and political actions."[9]

Mattina, though she is rich, does not belong to this world. The wealth she is seeking to acquire is "knowing" is non-materialistic. It is telling that she must go as far as possible from her own (U.S.) culture to find it, and that she dies so soon after realizing a truth:

> How far away you have been, and now your death is near; I hold in my hand the most distant star; the dead of yesterday dine with me at my table. (14)

Mattina's name is significant; "Mattina" means morning and "Brecon" sounds like "broken"; "Mattina Brecon" can be construed as "daybreak." Yet she dies of cancer, having come through her long night of searching, returning home after a nomadic existence. Mattina is interested in the Gravity Star, but it is not distance *per se* she is interested in, rather, the alienation from herself; from knowing the nature of her own humanity. Hene says to her: "When we do become far away from ourselves we become nothing. And if we are far from God, it's not God who does the abolishing, it's us." (84)

In other words, human-created spiritual meaning may be all there is beyond the physical world, but we are "nothing" without it. Mattina, even with all her wealth, has become thus alienated; perhaps it is her very wealth that alienates her? She has "everything," yet nothing: just what are the goods?

Peter's game is programmed in favour of "earth-weapons," the tools that have served humanity for a long continuum of time. Mattina searches for meaning not at home, but in "out-of-the-way" places where cultures have not been drastically changed. But the pristine beauty New Zealand is famous for, the environment humans depend upon for their well-being and survival is already under threat, as Hene tells Mattina. (88-9) Mattina, in best American philanthropic fashion, wants to solve the problems; Mattina should look to those of her own culture. Hene's comment is an example of people taking responsibility for themselves and their actions, a necessary step in the process of becoming an autonomous adult. Hene tells Mattina how the people on the marae have to make the kids feel important: "to love them, give them satisfying things to do." (88) This caring for others is implied to be the clue to a healthy future; people who feel loved will be secure in themselves, they will not need endless commodities to make them feel good, nor will they depend on the commodities of "drugs, glue, drink"--symbols of dependence on others and the wish to be in "another" state.

What, then, does Mattina find at the marae? It is poor materially; the houses are "bare bones, unclad, untiled, with old-fashioned sash windows, the cords hanging broken." (83) The people are poor, raising money to buy the pensioner flats from the Government through the slow business of competitions, games and the like. There are only six houses in the village; access is "poor" over an "uneven makeshift road"; (82) poverty is the key to this "important place" (87) where Mattina is nourished spiritually. The imagery of the passage where Mattina is eating is that of life, beauty, protection and strength. The marae is up stream, closer to the source, where the river is "clear blue and green and curve[s] closely against the earth like a greenstone necklace"; (82) the hill, with its "dark green wing" is protective like a great bird but not so much as to block the sun; children and dogs are playing, the old houses are like "the most ancient trees" and their walls cover them like "large faded aprons"--this last brings to mind a comforting, accepting mother-figure, always there, always ready to look after you providing you don't want fancy frills. Mattina feels the presence of a "yesterday's silence that [brings] a hunger to the back of her throat: a world-hunger." (85-86) Yet this is a woman of the world; why should she experience such a huge lack? It is significant, I think, that nowhere in this novel is Mattina's own mother mentioned, as though there has been a break in her experience of humanity's continuum.

The imagery just described combines old and new--the children, the old mother--just as the concept of communal living in harmony with Nature is at once an old and a new idea. The flax that Rua discusses (86) may represent nature; and Rua's "knowing" of it, the ability to use natural resources without destroying the environment they depend upon:

> "If [flax] won't grow for you, you can be sure you have hurt it."
> "Oh," Mattina said uneasily.

> "Flax is always alive. See this kete?"
>
> She held up a woven flax basket where she kept her sweater and pocketbook.
>
> "This is alive, listening to us now. Yes, you must have a special feeling about flax to be able to grow it, cut it without making it bleed, scrape it without hurting it, and weave it without going against its wishes."

"Sweater" and "pocketbook" are American terms, the usage of which is particularly apt for Rua's meaning, that the flax is listening, that there must be an acountability to nature. A "sweater" is also a worker, and a "pocketbook" could well be a book keeping a record of what (money) goes into the pocket. If natural resources (which may include humans) are being used for personal gain and not to fill real needs, as sweated labour in sweat shops is, following what are euphemistically known as "good business practices," then nature will retaliate; the flax won't grow. Need must be the motive, and loving care the mode, in the form of production that Rua espouses. Mattina responds "uneasily" to this "public mother" (86)--a metaphor for Mother Nature reprimanding the U.S. for the methods by which it and other capitalist economies accumulate their wealth? Most of Mattina's money comes from "Nana Connor's fortune"; (133) Nana Connor, the anaconda that crushes (oppresses) the life out of its prey.

It is traditionally women who tend the memories, who show the photographs, who remember the birthdays, who tend the gardens. On the marae, it is the oldest woman who calls *haere mai* when a stranger is to be welcomed.[12] Through their bearing of the children and their roles as the ones who care for the generation on either side of "this" one, women are more physically in touch--grounded--with the continuity of life. Madge McMurtrie's great-niece, Sharon, is pregnant, while Madge is about to die. (32) Madge gives Sharon her ring, of "real diamonds"; Sharon is "engaged now"--engaged in the continuity of birth and living and dying, her entitlement as a human being. Mattina's diamonds, that she has bought for herself, do not have this connotation of "real" worth (18, 170); rather, the bracelet and necklace give a sense of being manacles instead of ornaments.

Mattina is shackled to her life of entitlement of moneyed privilege, which has sheltered her from the real experiences of living. She had a nanny:

> like a near signpost along the distance to her parents, a port hostelry from which she returned to herself without making the complete journey to her parents. (75)

Likewise, Mattina engages Nanny Parker for her son John Henry. John Henry regards himself as "Nanny's real child" (142) and displays much anxiety about Nanny's love for him. Mattina's relationship with her child is presented as of a more trivial and unreal nature; he and she pursue a "fantastic 'chittering' [each night] about everything under the sun"; (171) she gives him chits, tokens for the real thing. By not giving him the full gift of herself, but substituting a Nanny, Mattina perpetuates the broken continuum of which she herself is a victim.

In thus breaking the continuum of nurturing, Mattina Brecon does damage to herself and her son. She feels alienated from him like a "spectator when she visit[s] the nursery . . . needing to have him translated by someone who knew his language." (136) Nanny Parker, though she loves John Henry, finds him precocious and is "amused by him as if he were a creature not part of the human race." (171) Jean Liedloff, in *The Continuum Concept*,[13] stresses how a child raised in tune with continuum principles has a sense of rightness, and will if each stage is handled appropriately grow into a responsible happy adult. John Henry "had fought long against growing up"; he looks older than his twenty years; he repeatedly reminds his parents of the chittering, that he wanted "as if the whole world depended on it." (170)

It is only at the very end of the book, the end result as it were, that John Henry, through an attention-getting strategy, wreaks mischief. Claiming to be narrator of *The Carpathians*. he wrenches the reader away from the sense of continuity experienced so far in the narrative, throwing into question its "truth." Such a device is an appropriate reminder that this is a work of fiction; yet readers familiar with the cultures described here will feel an undeniable recognition of the truths encoded in this work of art: "Art is a lie that makes us realize the truth."[14] The confusion of what is true within the narrative's own terms also aptly epitomizes the muddle of values in the modern world--who, or what, do we believe?

The New Zealand experience of colonization has been sufficiently damaging for this cautious statement to be made in a New Zealand nature journal:

> there are undesirable trends in New Zealand's population, in resource depletion, industrialization and environmental deterioration which cannot be ignored, for in dealing with nature many lessons have taught that prevention is simpler (and cheaper) than cure.[15]

Somewhat desperately, the writer pleads that the necessary planning "cannot be delayed." But the colonizing process continues, of overseas-generated technologies and ideologies. These have been planted in soil perhaps not conducive to their growth, else why would there be a need for articles such as "What's Really Wrong with New Zealand. . . ?" "The Country's in a turmoil," Hene says to Mattina on the marae: "we're in the kind of state where we now believe everything they tell us and absorb like blotting paper all their fine promises." (85) The blotting paper is a fine example of Frame's multi-purpose metaphors. It connotes bureaucracy, the hopes of the people being blotted out like the fine lines on blotting paper which blur until the words are indistinguishable; the words themselves read back to front on blotting paper, just as politicians so often go back on their promises, speaking a kind of double-talk; and the people themselves, blank-minded in their acceptance that the government knows best.

Rex Townsend, the "Full Gospel businessman" who brings his twice-widowed mother Connie Grant to Puamahara "for good," (91) doubtless knows what is best for her, even though Connie tells Mattina:

> I'll never get used to living here. They won't let me go home. And now they tell me they've bought me a flat, with my own money, mind you, and I'm moving in, two days from now, and I've got no things. Yesterday Dorothy took me to see that flat. They say there's not enough room here

> for me to stay. Then why did they send for me? I clean the house, I wash the breakfast dishes. I'm fussy about the bathroom, but Dorothy gets angry at the birdseed. (92)

In the light of previous death imagery, it is instructive to examine the Townsends a little more closely. The name "Rex" has connotations of kings, and of the flesh-eating dinosaur Tyrannosaurus Rex, both defunct species. When linked with Towns[-]end, the conclusion is that Rex's type and his habitat are on the way out. But Rex is a "Full Gospel businessman"; (23) surely an upstanding pillar of society? He works at night, however, as a "shift dyer," someone who changes things under cover of darkness, a shifty character. Dorothy obviously supports her husband in the decision to dump Connie into a flat, with her quibbling at Connie's attempts to do the housework. Could it be that this Full Gospel businessman has brought his mother here from England, so he can keep an eye on her money?--paying no heed to the trauma he has inflicted on her by doubly displacing her. Nothing but sound business practice, mind you, protecting an investment, as it were. But Rex and Dorothy must be kind people, surely? Dorothy has offered Mattina, the stranger, any help she needs; (22) Rex gives up his weekends to host meetings for young people in his garage. And they only play religious music, the sound of which will cover up anything else which might be going on within this "quiet" family keeping "[them]selves to [them]selves." (22-23)

Let Connie Grant, the "unclaimed" grandmother, (93) take up the story. Previous imagery lauding poverty should prepare the reader for Connie's role. She is "an elderly woman standing as if unsure what direction to take . . . thin, wearing a threadbare coat and carrying a shopping bag," with grey straggly hair, (183) whom Jake notices when Albion Cook the real estate agent is showing him his inherited property in Kowhai Street after Mattina's death. Jake is incredulous of Cook's story that everyone moved away at once, without warning, and approaches Connie for confirmation. When she tells him the details of how her family disappeared, Albion Cook tries to stop her. She continues to speak, despite his patronizing injunction: "'Now Connie, be careful what you say. you know you're only dreaming. You're not well. "Now Connie, be careful what you say. You know you're only dreaming. You're not well." Connie holds her ground, and Cook, "his feelings carefully concealed," attempts to regain control of the situation by constructing Connie as mad:

> It's better for us to go now . . . poor old Connie Grant. They let her stay in town, but believe me, she raves day and night about her so-called family in Kowhai Street. She couldn't believe they would shift house without telling her and then not get in touch with her. You'd be surprised what loving relatives do. Connie Grant will have to be put away, I fear!

Connie turns on Albion, calling him "a criminal" for not remembering her family. She tells Jake:

> I'm the only one now who remembers, the only one left. And it's a real memory. And I'm keeping it, I'm keeping it. And there was a woman here, an American like you, who escaped, she'll have the memory too, she took it with her; in her notebooks, in her bag, in her head, she won't lose it. She wrote it down on paper to be made into book. (184)

Connie clearly values the memory of the family; though they treated her badly, their memory is all she has left. She is poor, old and shabby, but she is rich in that she values her connection with humanity.

There are several binary oppositions being activated in the conflict between Connie Grant and Albion Cook: the masculine/feminine activities and modes of commerce and housework, aggression and submission, rationality and madness, centre and margin. The usual value placed on the first of each pair has been overthrown; the reader can assume Connie is not lying. The feminine attributes are thus brought in out of the cold. Why death? Much of this book stresses the spiritual death that much of modern "progress" brings, and in truly paradoxical style, must therefore die itself, or come to life, when opposites are overturned and near is far.

Turning the opposites around, it is Connie who has access to the *real* estate, the memory of Kowhai Street; memory is the "constant grant," the only estate humanity has title to. Albion (albino) Cook cooks the books, attempting to whitewash the truth about Jake's real estate. *The Oxford Dictionary of Quotations* lists a quotation attributed to Augustin, Marquis de Ximénèz: "Let us attack in her own waters perfidious Albion!"[16] Perfidious, treacherous Albion here is the enemy, the one to be frightened of, as Connie well knows, standing as he does for the lie that capitalism lives by: that we need it to survive.

But Connie is an "ordinary" citizen; who will speak for her? She ideally needs a voice to speak for her, to expose her story to the world. Connie tells Jake there was a woman, writing it all down, who would remember--or re/member. It is the writer who is the agent, the one who helps people with their *real* estate transaction--no mean job in a world that may have no meaning except what we give it. Reading this book, I found that people, their behaviour, and the everyday things of the world about me took on new meanings, became charged with significance. This is the job of the artist. The artists of New York City, the pioneers, gave it:

> shape and density . . . so that when outsiders looked at New York they saw not paper people in paper buildings under paper skies but real people of flesh and blood in an adamantine city of height and strength, of all dimensions. (104)

Far from fleecing the lambs as Albion Cook's kind does, the artist fleeces them with a comforting cover of meaning, a protection from the dangers "out there" in the "real" world, where death stalks in many forms.

The ending of *The Carpathians* is a kind of sudden, unexpected death. John Henry's disclaimer effectively "kills" the story, in one short paragraph. Perhaps this is a structural metaphor for the greatest threat of all to emanate from the imperial machine: annihilation by nuclear war. At a less dramatic level, John Henry's false alarm statement is similar to navigating one's way through a maze of traffic, only to be confronted with a "WRONG WAY--GO BACK" sign. The reader has been framed, a timely warning of the power of language. There is no magical way out in the direction we have been going; we need to go back to what we already know.

What we know, as John Henry reminds us, is everything,

and nothing. The autistic Decima makes circles with her arms, when her mother says: "There's no sign. Nothing." (106) When her father Joseph gives her a plastic snake, Decima "grabs it by the tail and describ[es] a circle" in response to their speaking to her. Decima's circles can be related to the message of good and evil, respectively the everything and the nothing, as found in the Bible. In a concordance to the Bible,[17] I found that the one mention of a circle in it is when the incomparableness of God is being lauded: "It is he that sitteth upon the circle of the earth, and the inhabitants thereof are as grasshoppers." (Isiah 40:22) The next verse mentions bringing "the princes to nothing," a reminder_that you can't take it with you, as they say. Decima's plastic snake-circle is the ouroborous, the symbol of the snake devouring itself with its tail in its mouth, its end in its beginning, a nice metaphor for the destruction of natural resources that capitalist society is undertaking: surely "the height of masochism and hunger."[18]

It is imagery, structure, irony and paradox, the art of writing, that is all-important in Frame's delivery of her message. her imagery, particularly, is of a global density so rich that every word counts and connects with all the others in a kind of literary ecology. But this construct of words is vulnerable, as the planet is proving to be; John Henry, boss now, has the power to censor it out of existence. Before it's too late, are the Carpathians any closer? The reader will remember the animals in this wild region, doubtless full of untapped resources: "the wolf, bear and lynx, the chamois and the ibex; the bearded vulture is found there." (66) The first three are Northern Hemisphere predators; the chamois's skin makes a good polishing cloth, to make things glossy, and along with the ibex the chamois approximates to prey and to relatives of the wild sheep; the bearded vulture is, according to the dictionary,[19] the "lammergeyer"; the largest European bird of prey, literally "lamb's vulture" from its preying on lambs. The Carpathians, "in crescent form," are, of course, none other than New Zealand, where, Frame appears to be saying, a more dangerous form of wilderness has overtaken the original. Whether the "tasting of the yesterday within the tomorrow" intimates that this situation will continue, or that looking back to yesterday may give answers for tomorrow in a paradoxical kind of revolution, is open to debate.

NOTES

1. Janet Frame, *The Carpathians* (London: Pandora, 1989).
2. Alan Wood, "What's Really Wrong with New Zealand and Why Australia is Different," *Weekend Australian*, 2-3 Nov. 1991, pp. 29-30.
3. A.L. Poole, "The Return of the Forests," *New Zealand's Heritage: The Making of a Nation*, 6 (1973), pp. 2342-47.
4. Toril Moi, *Sexual/Textual Politics: Feminist Literary Theory* (London: Methuen, 1985), p. 104.
5. Russell Ferguson, Introduction, *Out There: Marginalization and Contemporary Cultures*, ed. Russell Ferguson et al, Documentary Sources in Contemporary Art, 4 (New York: MIT, 1990).
6. Teresa L. Ebert, "Metaphor, Metonymy, and Ideology: Language and Perception in *Mrs. Dalloway*," *Language and Style*, 18.2 (1985), pp. 152-64.
7. A.W. Reed, *A Dictionary of Maori Place Names* (Wellington: Reed, 1961).
8. Janet Frame, *Owls Do Cry* (London: The Women's Press, 1985).
9. Teresa L. Ebert, p. 153.
10. I am indebted to my mother, Joan Lambert, for her help in deciphering meanings of characters's names: her memory from a lifetime of reading and a love of words proved invaluable.
11. Bell Hooks, *Ain't I a Woman: Black Women and Feminism* (Boston: South End, 1981).
12. Jill Stanbury, *Pers communication*, 10 November 1991.
13. Jean Liedloff, *The Continuum Concept* (Rev. ed., Harmondsworth: Penguin, 1986).
14. Picasso, quoted in Patrick Hughes and George Brecht, *Vicious Circles and Infinity: A Panoply of Paradoxes*. (Oxford: Blackwell, 1975), p. 69.
15. A.F. Mark, "Environment in Crisis," *New Zealand's Nature Heritage*, 1.1 (1974), pp. 4-8.
16. *The Oxford Dictionary of Quotations* (3rd ed., 1979).

17. Alexander Cruden, *Cruden's Complete Concordance to the Old and New Testaments* (London: Lutterworth, 1941).
18. Patrick Hughes and George Brecht, see illustrations.
19. *The Macquarie Dictionary* (2nd rev., 1987).

Postmodernist Strategies in Janet Frame's *Scented Gardens for the Blind*

VALERIE SUTHERLAND

Much of the writing of Janet Frame has been characterized as metafictional. As such it is centrally concerned with the psychological and social functions of language, and with narrative strategies. In the metafictional novel *Scented Gardens for the Blind*, Janet Frame postulates the essentially modernist principle that a definable transcendental truth exists which is not recoverable by humanity through normative behaviours or language. Paradoxically, in the very process of revealing the ultimate inability of language to reproduce this humanist essence, the novel casts into doubt the existence of such extra-linguistic truth. Early in the novel the character Vera Glace (who is in one sense the creator of the narrative and therefore speaks from a place close to the author herself) states: "I believe that each person's life contains one message which never reaches its destination. I deceive myself by thinking that I can repeat the message."[1]

Since the very notion of "message" is insubstantial and refers to linguistic transactions alone, it can be seen here, as elsewhere, that present in this text is the postmodern tenet that subjectivity is a construct of language. Aside from the central theme of linguistic philosophy, this novel is broadly (and deeply) concerned with social constructs, and the relationship between language and social power--a discussion to which constructions of gender are fundamental.

Modern psychoanalytical and feminist theories (notably those of Lacan, Kristeva and Irigaray), whilst differing in many particulars, all agree broadly on the simultaneity of, and isomorphic relationship between the development of language in the child and its social identity which is inevitably affected by gender.

The symbolic order, which is constituted by syntax, is entered through the "mirror phase": Lacan's explanation of the way an infant becomes aware of its separateness from the mother and other beings. Prior to entry into the symbolic order, the infant is said to be merged with the mother, to have no awareness of itself as social (or separate) being. Kristeva calls this pre-symbolic phase the semiotics. Simultaneous with becoming aware of itself as a being separate from others, is the development in the infant of language, that is, the ability to communicate through symbols and syntactically related signs. Entry into the symbolic order is said to mark the primary separation of the infant from the mother and to be a more or less painful experience.

Insofar as there is isomorphism between linguistic structures and social relations, the fixed rules of grammatical syntax are equivalent to the social laws of patriarchy in which the male term (the phallus) intervenes between the child and the matrix. Linguistically, what is thereby suppressed (the semiotic) includes all unruly methods of expression.

Feminist psychoanalysis proposes that social identity and language, requiring repression of the semiotic as they do, inevitably entail subservience to a patriarchal/phallic law which is repressive and exclusive. As Kristeva puts it, "women . . . seem to feel that they are the casualities, that they have been left out of the sociosymbolic contract, of language as the fundamental social bond."[2]

Some critical theorists (including Theresa Brennan, Susan Ash and Patricia Waugh) have questioned the assumption that this position of "nowhereness" cannot be overcome. They have raised the idea of a possible symbolic order which is not exclusive or repressive of the female voice, a pattern of coherence which does not conform to the linear logic of conventional patriarchal linguistic structures. The struggle for what might be termed a female symbolic entails some degree of rejection of what has come to be understood as the phallic symbolic, as Elizabeth Grosz puts it: "A language that is isomorphic with an autonomous, non-reductive femininity and pleasure, would have to overcome the domination and universalization of the masculine."[3]

The metafictional novel is a literary form through which a position antagonistic to patriarchal social order may be expressed. These works re-use and re-arrange the materials at hand. The structure of signification of the realist novel is reworked in such a way that it constitutes a critique of itself:

> Metafictional writers . . . turn inwards to their own medium of expression in order to examine the relationship between fictional form and social reality. They have come to focus on the notion that "everyday" language endorses and sustains . . . power structures through a continuous process of naturalization whereby forms of oppression are constructed in apparently "innocent" representations. The literary fictional equivalent of this "everyday" language of "common sense" is the language of realism. Metafiction sets up an opposition, not to ostensibly "objective" facts in the "real" world, but to the language of the realistic novel which has sustained and endorsed such a view of reality.[4]

The "naturalizing" impulse in the modernist novel is predicated on a notion that a universal "human nature" exists outside of history; this essentialist ideology reinforces the power structures of contemporary society by disguising them and de-naturalizing the experience of the socially marginalized. The representational text purports to use language as a cipher, the signs of which refer directly to pre-existing phenomena in the material world. When it comes to the modernist novel, the phenomenal subject of the enunciation is believed to be the consciousness of the author who uses language to convey his or her extra-linguistic experiences and ideas. Metafictional writing seeks to question this belief about the functioning of language--that language is a neutral instrument which enables the author to reveal essential truths which exist regardless of language. By separating the linguistic sign from a fixed referent, the non-representational (metafictional) text is able to focus on the sign itself in order to examine how language may construct consciousness rather than the reverse.

The relationship between language and consciousness is the major theme of *Scented Gardens* and in order to explore it thematically this novel (like *The Carpathians* and *Living in the Maniototo*) experiments with narrative strategies. Janet Frame uses metafictional elements to call into question both the naturalness and the acceptability of some of the social formulations of modern Western culture.

Susan Ash[5] has elucidated Janet Frame's concern with the position of the female artist as one in which there is no social place where a woman can both experience her social role as feminine and express her impulse as an artist. She characterizes the predicament as one in which in order to express her psychic reality a female artist must withdraw from social reality. The woman must either conform to social expectations of femininity (like the younger Malfred in *State of Siege*), i.e., become wife, mother, caregiver for the ill, teacher of the young etc., or become marginalized as mad. Patricia Waugh has pointed out that if women "speak outside [the symbolic] order they will either not be heard or be heard as insane."[6]

Ash discusses Janet Frame's feeling that society has left "no place on earth" for the female artist. This metaphor for the situation of the female artist may be extended to include all women who, to a greater or lesser degree, need to express their selfhood in a more satisfactory way than through the social roles allowed them by patriarchy. Whilst Susan Ash may be accurate in her summation that Janet Frame has survived as an artist "by removing [herself] from the conundrum"[7] by "a removal of self from the social and sexual arena"--she fails to acknowledge Frame's preparedness to engage in "radical meaning making." After having convincingly explicated the way in which Frame has condemned patriarchal society for its constriction of Malfred in *State of Siege*, she goes on to criticize her for a supposed resistance to an acknowledgement of patriarchy's culpability in the repression of the expressive impulse in women.

What is overlooked in Ash's thesis is the subversive nature of metafictional writing. If phallocentric linguistic structures allow the female voice nowhere to go, then new structures are required. *Scented Gardens* is largely about creating, or finding a "new language" which may at first be "understood by no-one and nothing," (10) and the postmodern elements in its form evidence Frame's preparedness to face "the conundrum" head on. If her social withdrawal has allowed her artistic survival, it has certainly not signalled capitulation. Rather it has marked a vigorous opposition to patriarchal power as manifested by the phallogocentric novel. Ash does not take into account that "language [can be] an important site of political struggle."[8]

Scented Gardens is a discourse on language--its structures, debasement, power; its relationship to subjectivity; and the way in which it is used to suppress, damage and obscure. Language is seen in this text as sustaining and mimicking an oppressive social order.

Unlike the realist novel, *Scented Gardens* does not subscribe to the illusion that language is a transparent, neutral medium for thought. On the contrary, it explores the materiality of language and its implication in producing and reproducing repressive social relationships and a debased culture. In this metafictional novel, Frame calls into question the validity of conventional writing (and reading) practice at the same time as using this practice to develop a pattern of coherence which breaks radically from the closed, linear narrative.

Scented Gardens uses a precisely ordered pattern of alternating perspectives. In fifteen chapters it repeats, five times, a cycle of narrative voice which begins with Vera Glace speaking in the first person, moves on to Erlene, whose interior monologue is couched in the third person, and thence to Edward, who is objectified in the third person voice. In the final chapter (16) we are moved out of the dramatization of interplay between the three protagonists (who think about each other but never actually occupy the same diegetic "space")[9] to be given the perspective of Dr. Clapper, whose revelations about Vera Glace place the preceding narrative as a construction of her fantasy. This narratorial switchback demands reflection on the reading process which is conventionally applied to the novel. This strategy of infinite regress (also used by Janet Frame in other novels) problematizes narrative authority. It foregrounds the process in reading of the desire for closure, the desire to know the point of origin. Since Dr. Clapper's account frames Vera's, it is privileged as the "truth," a proposition which does not bear much scrutiny. The reader is forced to acknowledge that the speaking subject is "empty outside of the very enunciation which defines it."[10]

Of course it is always true that the reader's identification with the protagonists of a novel has been manipulated by the author, and that the fictional world is an imaginative construction. In drawing attention to its own fictionality, *Scented Gardens* demonstrates the power of the habitual repression of the authorial voice in the modernist narrative.

The realist novel, and the critical practices consequent upon it, have trained the reader into complicity with the convention of denying, or at least masking, the source or the *enonce*[11] to such a degree that to have the mirror of representation turned back to reflect the habitual role of the reader in constructing the text can be disturbing. Like the quick drying paint that Vera sees advertised, this "habit sets . . . upon the mind, and one is grateful for this convenience the way it removes the need for laborious action or thought." (14)

When the text refuses to provide the "convenience" maintaining anonymity and absence of the creator of the narrative, the reader is called upon to participate overtly and actively in constructing meaning, and to be uncomfortably aware of this role.

The reflexive device is complex: whilst by the end of the novel we have placed Vera's as the constructing imagination, we are also aware that she herself is a construct of another imagination, the author's, which we must now recognize as obscured.

The infrastructure of the symbolic order in language is constituted by the syntagmatic chain whereby meaning can only be extracted from a series of words when they are placed in a pre-ordained relationship to each other. Meaning is transferred forward on a horizontal plane, and is thus contained within the complete sentence which is only meaningful because of the way the words are placed in relation to each other. In the syntagmatic chain, words stand in the place of phenomenal reality. Syntagmatic language strives to delete ambiguity and is therefore antagonistic to metaphor. It is the language of exchange: information is conveyed from one person to another with the least possible opportunity for there to be a difference between the message sent and that received. The signifier has a given signified.

Metaphorical language acknowledges the arbitrary nature of the connection between signifier and signified (word and meaning) and does not seek to fix the relationship between the two. Thus there is a degree of free play between the signifier and the various signified to which it may be attached, a "plurality of meaning."[12]

Scented Gardens is an exploration of a variety of discourses.

It establishes a conflict between the concatenation of syntagmatic language and the free play of metaphoric language. On one end of the spectrum is the language of "civilized" communication--words which are set in place by syntactical rules and which purport to communicate fixed meanings. On the other end is the primal cry of the beast which emerges, formless, from pre-history and is not understood as a system of fixed signifiers. Neither of these alternatives, the novel suggests, allows adequate understanding or empathy between human beings. At times the text appears to privilege non-syntactical language as more authentic, but ultimately it is shown to be an ineffective medium for communication.

Throughout the novel there are reverberations of two images which have been laid down as Vera's childhood memories. The first is her infantile elaboration of a nursery rhyme, recited by her mother, in which a "huddle of beggars" are kept at bay outside in the dark by "menacing dogs." This archetypal image of the socially marginalized crystallizes the response of normative society to "hunger and misery" (of all types), and that is to fear and deny it--to silence effectively its victims. The lack of communication with those who are perceived as other is characterized as immaturity. The question is asked: "How soon shall we learn to break the silence and speak to them." (50)

The second paradigmatic image is that of the lighthouse keeper whom Vera, as a child, sees on the beach. He has gone mad and is being subdued by two men who are taking him away to an asylum. What lasts in Vera's memory is his "high-pitched scream," like that of a seabird, which seems to signify to her a great freedom and she imagines that he "had [indeed] changed to a seabird." (45) He hasn't, of course, and the image of a screaming madman locked away by other men is, for the reader, a powerful one of lack of freedom. The lighthouse keeper had been living outside of interactive society; "deprived of most of the amenities of civilization, he remained, they said, one of the happiest men alive." (45) The ironic insertion of this comment's source ("they said") underscores ambivalence toward any notion that isolation from society and release from normative social and linguistic laws constitute of themselves, freedom.

And then there is the materiality of language in *Scented Gardens*. Several fully elaborated metaphors evoke images of words as plants, either gone to seed or pruned, as putrescent waste, as aggressive flying insects. For Edward, communicating in words is what maintains humanity. He felt that people "were in danger of becoming cripples of loneliness and silence with their language decayed, the words overgrown and no longer cared for, not pruned or picked, or marketed, arranged in shining bowls in shaded rooms of the mind." (133)

In opposition to Edward's rank, unweeded garden of careless language, Erlene imagines the language of poetry in which "words in a language, nouns, verbs, adverbs, sentences [are] clipped like hedges and lawns into strange shapes that surprise you in the dark? Sentences with the growth cut back." (180) Remembering her school experiences with poetry, Erlene recalls the

> Honors Board where each year in the long summer holidays . . . the latest names were added in gold lettering which did not seem quite dry . . . as if, had they rubbed their sleeves against the name, it would have been obliterated, or the letters would have curled up and dropped from the wall as no name, nothing but shavings of gold paint. And that showed how easily words could be torn, distorted, made unrecognizable, or removed altogether. (108)

Here, as elsewhere in the novel, there is a suggestion that words and naming--the articulation of the symbolic order--is an unreliable way of fixing or defining reality. In fact, in Erlene's experience, certain types of verse are used to obscure the truth and distort reality. In a school text she reads:

> Far are the shades of Arabia
> Where the princes ride at noon.
> But Erlene was old enough to know that it was not like that anymore, it had never been like that, there was all disease and desert and fighting and hunger. (58)

Erlene's metaphor of the well-clipped garden of poetic language changes as she elaborates her terror of being unable to communicate in language, and words become flying insects which:

> cluster like flies about her, and lay little white eggs upon her. (227)

Vera fears the isolation of being the only person left on earth with the capacity to use language:

> I shall find heaps of decaying words on the sides of the road, in gutters, in rubbish dumps and litter bins, for every home will have cast out words as useless. (216)

Syntagmatic language is seen as an affectation of an over-sophisticated metropolitan civilization which has lost meaning because it has lost touch with an ancestral, primeval past. Erlene imagines being the vector of a dehumanized "ancestral voice," a "true sound" which would be "the ultimate denial of cities and people and rich stores of language skimmed century after century from the settled civilizations of human beings." (227)

This lost past would seem to have something in common with the pre-oedipal unconscious (the semiotic) which is repressed by the interdiction of the symbolic. Erlene is identifying her disempowerment, her inability to express her poetic self, as being the result of centuries of Western culture--which is marked by patriarchy.

The central protagonist of *Scented Gardens* (Vera/Erlene) experiences hysterical aphasia. In Lucen Irigaray's view:

> hysteria can be seen as the woman's rebellion against and rejection of the requirements of femininity . . . an attempt to return nostalgically to the pre-oedipal, homosexual desire for the mother . . . the hysteric refuses heterosexual passivity and the sexual compliance with social norms by transferring sexual intensity and meaning into her symptoms.[13]

Erlene's aphasia is seen in the novel as a rejection of the adulterated discourses available in the social world, "the tattered bargain-priced words, the great red-flagged sale of trivialities." (12) While she refuses to interact within the verbal exchange systems of the society around her, her silence constitutes another type of discourse, beyond even that of inarticulate sound. Her silent presence is a statement of resistance to the symbolic order as it is available to her. In Irigaray's thesis, the hysteric "articulates a corporeal discourse; her symptoms speak" on her behalf.[14] Erlene's discourse of silence signifies disgust with and mistrust of the conventional discourses which others comply with unquestioningly.

Erlene's silence threatens her parents, it forces them to "face their own reflections." (87) Edward, the father, is the one most endangered by his daughter's resistance to social convention. He has spent years charting the genealogy of an arbitrarily chosen family. The historical chronicle, being one of the most highly rigidified discourses, conforms to standard rules and pins down into static display what has been the life of the past, "the dead are put in their place," as though by fixing historically a human "chain," the effect of time could be resisted or denied.

Fantasizing and experiencing power vicariously as director of his toy regiments and his "beautifully typed, bound and filed" chronicles, Edward's narrative in the novel, explores the relationship between the reality of lived experience and the abstract, linguistic construction of an imaginary life. For Edward it is the *form* of conventional language and discourses which is important; he does not care what is being said, so long as orderly communication is apparently taking place. Ironically he eventually comes to experience the disembodied, truly chaotic voices of his schizophrenia as more "real" than the spoken words of people around him:

> The voices nagged him at night . . . [they] talked trivialities. . . . Or they called his name. . . . At other times the voices spoke obscenities about the Strang family . . . however he decided to act, Edward could not ignore the voices. They claimed his consciousness as if it belonged to them by right . . . only when they had withdrawn could he make some movement. (197)

Whilst Edward is in the thrall of the voices, his housekeeper wakes at night to hear him "trying to catch the voices as they withdrew beyond the range of his reply--his abuse, argument, entreaty." (201) His daughter's refusal to speak in words constitutes a threat to his arrangement of the human race in "a follow-my-leader of chains." (105) The suggestion is that if language can be ordered into a coherent chain and thereby be inscribed with meaning, then human existence also needs a universally coherent order to be meaningful. The ironical treatment of Edward and the ultimately vacuous nature of his chronicle of the Strang family suggests a dismissal of his theory. The list of unattached terms and phrases from the "book on Practical Speech Training" (104) needs to be fixed into a structure in specific relation to each other and "it is a treacherous path from incoherence to lucidity," (104) and vice versa. As with the man imprisoned in Socrates's metaphorical cave, who is suddenly unchained and is able to look at that which he has previously been able to understand through its name only, Edward finds that "Outside of language, outside of convention and communal recognition, outside of identical perception that can be identified within a set of procedures for conversation with others who share his view, these things are for him nothing."[15]

It is this structure of the symbolic order which threatens Erlene. Within her protective dome of silence, she is free to explore a relationship with the imaginary faerie world--a discourse of childhood and connection with the mother. She retreats into this world (where Uncle Blackbeetle satisfies her need for communication) in order to avoid the transition into adulthood in a social world which would insist upon her acceptance of a role designated by external forces, on her acceptance of heterosexual, socially constructed femininity.

When she "accidentally" breaks her silence with Dr. Clapper, her link with her imaginary is severed and Uncle Blackbeetle dies. She imagines she has been sexually penetrated and is pregnant to Dr. Clapper. Kristeva points out in *Women's Time* that "Women are increasingly describing their experience of the violence of the symbolic contract as a form of rape." (43)

In an attempt to retreat from adult heterosexuality and the symbolic contract, Erlene wishes to return to her schoolgirlhood, but she remembers that

> the sixth-form room was at the same time filled with terror, and all could feel it when week by week news came that one of the girls--in turn Molly or Beatrice or Helen--was planning to leave school, or had left already to take up

> nursing or to work in the farmer's co-op or in the post office. . . . But they all feel stifled there and smiled to each other and said, What fun, I wish I were out in the world earning . . . like Molly and Beatrice and Helen. (231)

The socializing procedures of the school place further obstacles between the child and its pre-oedipal identity. This repressive training is most marked in the teaching of speech and language. Verses packaged within the classroom are neat, hackneyed rhymes, used to train the speaker through rote repetition and leached of evocative power.

In this exploration of the various qualities and functions of syntactical language, unstructured utterances, and silence, *Scented Gardens* identifies the parameters of a struggle for a non-phallic symbolic, a pattern of coherence which is not conditional on silencing the semiotic/ feminine. Patrick Evans points out:

> In the world of Vera Glace there is [great] concern with the possibility that human beings may contain a latent capacity to communicate in a new way, from beyond the alphabet. . . . Thematically, [*Scented Gardens*] is constantly devoted to the problem of finding this language which will "saw through the bars, the mile-wide walls" created by everyday language.[16]

Evans interprets the nuclear holocaust and Vera's primeval utterance at the end of the novel as a proposition that a "purgation" is required before "a truly human voice" can emerge. It is highly probable that one of Janet Frame's overriding concerns is the inauthenticity of everyday language of communication. What is less clear is whether she is arguing for an essential, "true" humanity which is anterior to language, or whether her work corroborates the postmodern theory that language "actually dictates and circumscribes what can be said and therefore what can be perceived."

It is true that her character's perceptions of themselves are developed independently of spoken, syntactical language, but is she struggling to express a modernist idea of subjectivity in a postmodernist structure? Or are Janet Frame's works examples of the semiotic "transgressing its boundaries"[17] in the linguistic field?

The breakdown of social identity which results in psychosis is analogic to the breakdown of linguistic coherence which results in Vera's "new language" of bestial sounds. However, as Elizabeth Grosz points out,[18] another result of the semiotic breaking through the carapace of the symbolic is poetry--the coherence of metaphor and ambiguity.

There is considerable irony in Vera/Erlene's first and final utterance being interpreted as a "new" language. It is only after the atom bomb has been dropped on England that this psychotic mute, for the first time in 30 years, sits in a chair and looks human. If the unintelligible sounds she utters represent the beginnings of a new language of humanity, then surely the point is that Western civilization has entered into barbarism.

Janet Frame's struggle for a "new," more authentic language (a struggle carried on through several other novels) is more progressive than Evans suggests. *Scented Gardens* does not valorize Vera's voice from "out of ancient rock and stone" (252) any more than it authenticates the hackneyed banalities of conventional, univocal discourse. The difficulty is, this novel suggests, for language to go beyond:

> mere animal cries, demands for food, warmth, love . . . human pleas for forgiveness, salvation, peace of mind . . . [and to find] the speech which arranges the dance and pattern of the most complicated ideas and feelings of man in relation to truth; it, the center, the circus, the crack of the whip, the feeding ground of the spirit. (53)

In proposing that hysterical resistance is ultimately self-defeating, and rigorous conformity repressive and alienating, the novel does not present an atavistic vision. It does affirm, through both form and content, the fundamental role played by language in human consciousness and to that extent, despite the fact that its creation pre-dates much of what is thought of as postmodernist critical theory, *Scented Gardens* is a consummately metafictional work.

NOTES

1. Janet Frame, *Scented Gardens for the Blind* (London: The Women's Press, 1982), p. 48.
2. Julia Kristeva, *Women's Time*.
3. Elizabeth Grosz, *Sexual Subversions* (North Sydney: Allen and Unwin, 1989).
4. Patricia Waugh, *Metafiction--The Theory and Practice of Self-Conscious Fiction* (London: Methuen, 1985), p. 11.
5. Susan Ash, "Janet Frame: The Female Artist as Hero," *Journal of New Zealand Literature*, No. 6, 1988.
6. Patricia Waugh, *Feminine Fictions*, p. 59.
7. Susan Ash, p. 186.
8. Chris Weedon, *Feminist Practice and Poststructuralist Theory* (Oxford: Basil Blackwell, 1987), p. 24.
9. That is to say, they never actually "meet" as part of the story. Since, as we eventually discover, the three are aspects of one character's imagination, this detail carries some significance.
10. Roland Barthes, *Image/Music/Text* (Great Britain: Fontana/Collins, 1977), p. 145.
11. That is, the "subject of the enunciating." See *Literary Theory--An Introduction* by Terry Eagleton (Oxford: Basil Blackwell, 1983), p. 169.
12. Chris Weedon, p. 24.
13. Elizabeth Grosz, p. 134.
14. *Ibid.*, p. 135.
15. Lucen Irigaray, *Speculum of the Other Woman*, p. 272.
16. Patrick Evans, *Janet Frame* (Boston: Twayne, 1977), p. 110.
17. Grosz, p. 48

Keri Hulme's *The Bone People* and *Te Kaihau:* Postmodern Heteroglossia and Pre-textual Play

SUZETTE HENKE

In her prize-winning novel *The Bone People*, Keri Hulme attempts to do what has never been done before: she writes a modern Maori epic that voraciously absorbs, assimilates, and transforms the literary heritage of both east and west--Maori culture and European myth, tribal allegory and Joycean epic. Critics have been quick to compare her writing to the rugged, individualistic, American prose of Ernest Hemingway or Norman Mailer. Hulme's protagonist Kerewin Holmes, a tough-minded and hard-drinking isolee, may well be a female version of the Hemingway hero, complete with boozy stream-of-consciousness monologues and acerbic eruptions of self-flagellating prose. Stylistically, however, Hulme's paradigms stray far from the taut, laconic utterances of the *macho* male of North American literary fame.

I would like to suggest that Hulme's stylistic forebears might be found at the opposite end of the literary spectrum--not in the spare, taut style of Ernest Hemingway or of her New Zealand contemporary Janet Frame, but in the epic capaciousness of Shakespeare, Dante, Rabelais, and Joyce. In *The Bone People*, Hulme constructs an epic of prodigious dimensions. Like Joyce's *Ulysses*, it confines itself to the microcosmic purview of three different minds: Kerewin Holmes, Simon P. Gillayley, and his foster-father Joseph N. Gillayley.

The configuration of characters is different, but the triadic paradigm (inverted) is similar, in a number of ways, to that of *Ulysses*. Both Joyce and Hulme are constructing a massive epic of the human body that will encompass the bowels of compassion

(Jewish Bloom/Maori Joe); the detached artistic/philosophical head, erudite but unloving (Stephen Dedalus/Kerewin Holmes); and the sensuous, inarticulate body of (M)other love, raging with inchoate drives channelled into an endlessly deferred and disseminated longing (Molly Bloom/Simon Gillayley). In each of these epics, head, heart and body remain isolated in their discrete preoccupations, but eventually fuse and are synthesized into a powerful communal myth of love and satisfaction.

Keri Hulme deliberately reconstructs and redistributes traditional sex-roles. Her female hero is a figurative tower of strength, "Kerewin the stony," who inadvertently supports and becomes emotionally attached to the adoring males in her charge. It is Kerewin, the female artist, who proves master of the different kinds of knowledge and power traditionally associated with the artist, the shaman, the priest, the wizard, and the witch. Like Joyce's Stephen Dedalus, she envisages herself as a priest of art, transubstantiating the daily bread of human experience into the ever-living life of painting and fabulation. And like Shakespeare's Prospero. she has access to arcane, seemingly magical powers--both psychic, through the imaginative evocation of fabulative other-worlds; and physical, through the practice of Japanese martial arts. Joseph Gillayley, in contrast, functions as Hulme's Everyman: he resembles the humbler, more docile, but healthily curious Leopold Bloom, whose vast store of semi-accurate knowledge has been acquired through the university of life. And Simon, the *infans* of the story, is vaguely analogous to Molly Bloom whose seething, swirling consciousness ranges over the Dublin landscape and occasionally mourns the infant son lost eleven days after birth.[1]

James Joyce initially set out to Europeanize Irish literature and, like his hero Stephen Dedalus, to forge in the smithy of his soul the uncreated conscience of a disturbingly provincial, xenophobic, and incestuously inward-looking Irish race. Similarly, Keri Hulme wants to redefine Maori and Pakeha culture simultaneously--to offer a written testament to the rich oral history of her people, an epic that will embrace a thousand years of European literary myth at the same time that it celebrates the communal triumph of Maori interdependence.

Hulme's female protagonist is a light-skinned octoroon, one-eighth Maori on her mother's side. Joseph (Hohepa) Gillayley is a dark-skinned aboriginal. And his foster-child Simon Peter (Haimona) is a fair-haired, blue-eyed boy of European origins, half-Irish and half-French (though we do not learn this, conclusively, in the text of the novel). Like Joyce, Hulme celebrates an adoptive/spiritual parenthood in lieu of biological affiliation. And she suggests, at the end of the book, that all three worlds--Maori, Pakeha, and European--can come together in rich, finely tempered, triumphant amalgamation.

> They were nothing more than people, by themselves. Even paired, any pairing, they would have been nothing more than poeple by themselves. But all together, they have become the heart and muscles and mind of something perilous and new, something strange and growing and great.
>
> Together, all together, they are instruments of change.[2]

The play of experimental language is central to Keri Hulme's finely crafted prose, which unfolds in a rich heteroglossia, a stream-of-consciousness style that moves from the mind of Kerewin Holmes through the seething perceptual world of Simon P. Gillayley, to the enraged, fragmented, and chaotic mental landscape of his intermittently abusive stepfather Joe.[3]

Surely Yeats and Joyce are present as ghostly absences when Kerewin builds her tower of stone, topped with a "star-gazing platform" and harbouring at its centre "a quiet library, book-lined, with a ring of swords on the other wall." (7) One thinks of W.B. Yeats's Thoor Ballylee at Gort and of Yeats's paternal prayer for his daughter Anne, begging that she be blessed with the grace of a self-delighting, self-appeasing, self-affrighting life. "No need of people," thinks Kerewin, "because she was self-fulfilling, delighted with the pre-eminence of her art." (7) Her thoughts of joy at aesthetic isolation more closely resemble the sociopathic misanthropy of Joyce's Stephen Dedalus, incarcerated in a colonial Martello Tower at the beginning of *Ulysses*. Kerewin thinks:

> But the pinnacle became an abyss, and the driving joy ended. At last there was a prison.
>
> I am encompassed by a wall, high and hard and stone, with only my brainy nails to tear it down. (7)

For Stephen, too, the tower becomes a Celtic prison in which he is mocked by a stage Irishman and interrogated by an English interloper.

Towers, of course, have a long history of medieval lore and western, Eurocentric mythic meaning. European culture is rife with legends of Arthurian knights whose prowess is linked to that ancient symbol combining phallic strength with womb-like interiority. But modern literature has culled from this symbol darker, more haunting myths of incarceration unto death: the Dantesque tale of Ugolino and his children, immured in a tower that will serve as their tomb; and of T.S. Eliot's use of Ugolino's trial as a metaphor suggestive of contemporary solipsism--the modern *malaise* of narcissism unto (social/communal) death. Even the medieval Fisher King remains present as an absence buried at the heart of a religious darkness impenetrable to the poetic pen/phallus/sword. The unreal towers of Jerusalem, Athens, and Alexandria are falling and bursting in the violet air of Eliot's *Waste Land*. In Keri Hulme's Maori epic, the tower as an isolated hermitage will eventually be destroyed, to be replaced by the large communal mead/hall and memory/hall where the entire tribe can gather in a festive, phoenix-like dance of resurrection.

When Kere first sees Simon Gillayley, she is startled by the appearance of a fairy form, an angelic sylph whose gender seems indeterminate:

> In the window, standing stiff and straight like some weird saint in a stained gold window, is a child. A thin shock-headed person, haloed in hair, shrouded in the dying sunlight.
>
> The eyes are invisible. It is silent, immobile. (16)

This apparition turns out to be Simon, the boy who cannot speak--the ratbag of a child whose throat has been stopped by physical and psychological trauma; the demonic being whose devilish, autistic outbursts cloak a Christ-like figure in ghost-haunted silence and make him "a bit of an outlaw." (49)

This waif has been rescued from shipwreck by Joseph N. (of Nazareth?) Gillayley, whose name suggests biblical nuances of another foster parentage that ended in bloody crucifixion. Joe, the warm-hearted, semi-literate Maori who has lost Hana his wife and Timote, the child of his body, represents the strong, passionate, irascible heritage of post-colonial impotence. Joe lavishes paternal care on his Aryan charge and loves the speechless *infans* with such powerful ferocity that he hugs, handles, nurtures, and beats him as mood (and alcoholic irascibility) dictate. Inscribed in the impotence and frustration of a colonized and indigent race, Joe plays the role of foster-father and near-executioner in this allegorical tale of sin, repentance, purgation, and resurrection.

> Joseph Nothing Gillayley.
> Literate. Tidyminded. Widower. . . .
> Put "tidyminded" with "drink" and you get the rigid dignity-on-a-high-horse that intensely dislikes anything or anyone getting out of the way. The dedicated drinker of this sort never gets messily drunk. Nastily, but not messily.
> Focus the picture again. Not a roaring Viking. A pale cold-eyed man who expects too much of his offspring so the offspring goes defensively wild.
> The long hair didn't fit, though. Nor did the scarecrow appearance. Nor the maternal sympathy, ease-up child, the little man showed. Or the boy's readiness to get near a stranger. (45)

Simon is the "jetsam" cast adrift in a terrible, Labour weekend out-of-season storm, when a mysterious cruiser was shipwrecked off Ennetts Reef. "Everybody aboard came ashore. One way or the other." (51)

> He was almost literally black and blue all over from cold and bruising. I didn't know it till after, but his left hand was smashed, his left arm broken in two places, three ribs on that side were fractured, and both his collarbones were cracked. Like he had hit something very hard, arm first. I just picked him up, wrapped him in my coat, and ran back, was blown back, shouting like a lunatic with the wind cutting into my kidneys like a knife. And after that, everything is a bit blurred. The ambulance ride into Taiwhen-

> uawera with two corpses for company. Long waiting, or it seemed like it in hospital rooms with huge bright lights. Examinations, and him screaming his head off. He seemed to come back to life very quickly. Scared as hell, but even when he was half-conscious, he was clinging like a leech to my hand all the time he could and they'd let him. Shock, exposure, pneumonia, he should be dead, said the hospital, and enumerated the breaks. (85-86)

This hapless orphan, washed ashore in *Tempest*-like fashion, remains an enigmatic figure at the heart of Keri Hulme's narrative. He bears, as his heritage, a luxurious rosary made of precious stones and a gold earring signifying epicenes or exotic origins. Simon's skin is cream-coloured, like Kere's; his earring suggests an androgynous bearing, an aesthetic history buried with his nameless parents; and his ear, not (yet) deaf, responds uncannily to the utterance of French phrases. Does the earring signify an aristocratic lineage or a past enslavement? And what kind of masochistic history pushes the child toward resigned submission to his adoptive father's obsessive beatings? The victim has ironically defined himself as guilty and worthy of barbarous recrimination. He internalizes the rage and the beatings and connives with his stepfather to hide a mutual, and muted, pain. Who but a female hero could rescue this battered goblin-soul?

A plethora of riddles inhabits *The Bone People*--mysteries never clarified or resolved in the text. "Another thing used to be Citroen cars. He had a bee in his bonnet about them for some reason. And fires. . . . Those beads were his lucky talisman for over a year. . . . They were in the pocket of the woman's blouse." (87) The name "Clare" resounds like a metronome through the boy's inchoate internal monologue. The unuttered syllable dominates his pre-Oedipal emotional landscape and resonates with insatiable notes of infantile longing. The mystery of Simon's origins functions as an aporia in the fragmented, decentered narrative of Keri Hulme postmodern epic.

In *The Bone People*, Hulme, it seems, has produced a fictive equivalent of Shakespeare's *Tempest* and placed a female Prospero at its fabulative centre. Like Prospero, Kerewin Holmes, by the end of the novel, exposes Simon's origins and wins the goblin child as prize of her heart. But the central question is never answered. Was Timon, the weird singer and heroin addict whom Joe heard about in the Maori outback, somehow related to the speechless boy? The songs that Timon croons would suggest some connection; but strange European ghost-figure remains a loose end in the text, part of a subplot never tied up in neat denouement. Why was this grotesque drug-addict wandering Maori tribal lands? And was he, like some spectre out of a Dickens novel, Simon's long-lost father? Only Keri Hulme knows for sure. And she refuses to tell us until the publication of *The Bone People*'s "pretext," "A Drift in Dream," one of the short stories included in *Te Kaihau/The Windeater*.[4]

In true Joycean fashion, Keri Hulme has not only given us "The End at the Beginning" in the form of a prologue; she has also reserved the aporetic kernel of her *Tempest*-uous drama for post-epic publication in a future collection of stories. Such playful, invaginated intertextuality expands the self-reflexive postmodern mode to embrace and enfold the canonical unity of its author's fabulative god-games. Kerewin Holmes may appear to emulate the magical powers of Prospero, that Shakespearean Shaman who controls the purgation and salvation of a royal, shipwrecked crew. All along, however, Kerewin has been stumbling through a house of distorting mirrors, a postmodern field of play controlled by an authorial puppet-master always-already present in the mode of mocking, Maori dream-keeper. Like Shakespeare's Prospero, Kerewin Holmes appears to be manipulating an artistic drama on an island-continent in an epic tale. But, as it happens, it is she herself who, along with Joe and Simon, eventually proves to be the object of a series of "god-games" manipulated from some inscrutable, other-worldly stage.[5]

We only learn of Simon's family history in the highly evocative short story, "A Drift in Dream," published in *Te Kaihau/The Windeater*. It is here that the child's French mother, Marie-Clare de Vraiencourt, appears like a tawdry version of Shakespeare's Miranda: "I have been in the world four hours," she mutters, as she encounters the society of men for the first time in her adult life.[6] So long shielded from sexual desire and social reality, the ex-nun finds herself emerging, at the age of thirty-six, into a strange and wondrous male-dominated world that both intrigues and terrifies her. A thin, ascetic, saintly character, she plays Ariel to Timon/Liam's drug-debauched Caliban.

In her portrayal of Timon Padraic McDonnagh, a.k.a. Liam, Hulme may, ironically, be drawing on late nineteenth-century British colonial myths of Irish evolutionary debasement. To the upper-class Englishman contemptuous of Celts inhabiting John Bull's other island, the impoverished Irish seemed members of a different species--simian ancestors or gibbous missing links, but certainly not intellectually evolved, fully cognizant and dignified human subjects. As the Maoris were to the Pakehas, so the Irish appeared to their English colonizers. What better figure could occupy the marginalized subject-position of the Caliban-like Other than a debazed remnant of the 1960s counterculture--an Irish hippy addicted to mind-altering drugs?

Longhaired and androgynous, Timon Padraic McDonnagh has the "slanting green eyes" of a foreigner or a devil and first appears, in androgynous guise, as a neuter subject of indeterminate gender: "It is a man, she thinks. It has long hair drawn back from a highboned face." (*TK*, 193) His grin reveals the "white and beautiful teeth" of a fox or a shark. Yet, like a sleek animal, he is sensuously attractive; there is a fluid, beautiful grace about his movements. He is even perceived as a "gaudy angel" and saviour to Marie-Clare lost in the crush of a threatening mob.

A cross between Ariel and Miranda, Marie-Clare constructs her own subject position in terms of Christian asceticism and the patient endurance of pain. She sees herself in saintly guise, as a cheerful martyr in the face of adversity: "I am considered strong. Remember the winter when your feet cracked open but you still walked the frosty ground, leading your sisters in laying the concrete blocks for the new dormer? All the while laughing when laughter was needed, because the pain was nothing beside the love burning in your heart?" (*TK*, 194) Like Shakespeare's Miranda, she has been sheltered from the world of men and finds herself immediately attracted to the first male she sees after her (re)birth into the chaotic, bustling crowd of an urban metropolis.

Like Maria, the dogged and demeaned spinster of Joyce's short story "Clay," Hulme's Marie has been working in the laundry business. The Maria of *Dubliners* is a shy celibate labourer in the Dublin-by-lamplight Laundry, a home for reformed (Protestant) prostitutes; in contrast, Marie-Clare has embraced celibacy as a Nun/laundress in a Catholic monastery--

a term that would indicate her indentured servitude to ecclesiastical patriarchy. After twelve years in service to the Church, this Bride of Christ relinquishes the "pleasures and pangs of God" to pursue the "human fire" of amorous passion. An intact virgin, she seeks not sex, that phallic *con*-junction that she has never actually known; but rather, the emotional *con*-summation of sensuous communion with a fellow spirit: "I need . . . to hold. To be held" (*TK*, 195).[7]

Liam/Timon, a longhaired member of the sixties's counterculture, inhabits a semi-lyrical, semi-debased world of sex, music, and dreams. If this Irish Caliban wallows in a drugged stupor, he nonetheless emerges as an Ariel-like singer, a Celtic bard who embraces Marie-Clare as a "fellow musician" and angelic agent of (spiritual? financial?) "salvation." (*TK*, 196) Although Liam sings beautifully, he is a subject bereft of words and languishing in smoke-filled, bleary-eyed consciousness. Apart from the songs he so joyfully croons, his own powers of articulation have degenerated into the half-mute, monosyllabic utterances of beatnik *argot*. When Liam's friend Paddy, for instance, feels exhilarated by Marie's angelic music-making, he can only utter squeaks of profane pleasure: "Shit, like wow. Shit." (*TK*, 197)

A postmodern amalgamation of Ariel and Caliban, Liam/Timon seems like an adolescent sylph, "slim and straight and golden" (*TK*, 197)--the magician who concocts a dizzying potion of peppermint tea fit for the gods. His history remains dark, shadowy, violent, and traumatic. An escape from a "bog of a castle" presided over by a gnarled gnome of a grandfather who "stamps and snarls" like a mythic dragon or equine monster, Liam, the "whoreson" of a lunatic "bitch" can, like Caliban, utter only curses in the delineation of his spawning. Hence the malicious oath: "My grandfather may his soul rot a thousand years in torment." (*TK*, 198) As the unwanted son of a half-mad daughter-in-law, Liam, like a Shakespearean bastard, has been barbarously socialized in practices of "sabotage and hate" against his paternal lineage.

Despite his comradery with a rowdy, Antipodean crew , Liam is capable of surprising asceticism. He waits patiently, like a knight of old, or like Prince Ferdinand playing chess with his beloved Miranda, for the voluntary bequest of his lady's hand. Marie-Clare, fed on green wine and magical potions, grows younger in spirit until she loses the weight of years and buoyantly doffs the chains of her celibacy. Her counterculture Prince Charming puts her to sleep with soporific drugs, then kisses her into sexual awakening. He feels, triumphantly, that he has seduced an adulterous Bride of Christ: "O it was the stuff of legends," he boasts. "I have taken God's bride and she is more pleased with me." (*TK*, 199)

Behind Liam's serene and sensuous lovemaking, however, lurks a frightening, bestial capacity for violence--the unpredictable irascibility of an angry, wounded, battered, and battering male. He had tried, after all, to incinerate his grandfather in the ancestral castle that so tarnished his youth. Later, at a party, he kicks a (pregnant?) woman in the stomach, apparently without motive. Only morphine can mitigate this modern-day Caliban's "angry and impotent rage." (*TK*, 204)

By the end of the story, a road accident has extinguished Marie-Clare's Ariel spirit. The patriarchal (phallic) thumb of Liam brutally gags his son's first infantile iteration, "Maman?":

> he swings round catches hold of a hand a throat and shouts as he bends "Don't talk of her! . . . O God a life for a life is fair but not her you have me now that's fair for I watched the pulse in his throat flick and die under my thumb but not her don't ever talk of her!"
>
> He says to the gagging huddle on the floor, "For the fire of God has got her and shall come for us all." (*TK*, 205-6)

In fury, Liam strangles the uncomprehending child, reducing him, through physical injury or psychic trauma, to a permanently dumb, autistic figure.

Thus Simon P. Gillayley's dramatic childhood history unfolds, paradoxically, in a narrative pre-text that succeeds its epic iteration. At the end of the *Windeater* story, "A Drift in Dream," Simon and Liam are about to embark on their fateful journey to New Zealand waters and to a *Tempest*-like purgation off the coast of a new world. Marie-Clare's religious name, *Soeur Bonaventure*, comes back to haunt this ill-starred family, whose peace has twice been shattered by accidents on land and sea. Certainly, Keri Hulme is generically indulging in what Northrop Frye would call a "romance" rather than a "novel." In true Dickensian fashion, the plot is littered with improbable coincidences, melodramatic accidents, and paradigmatic experiences of death and resurrection.

Like the drowned Phoenician sailor in Eliot's *Waste Land*; or like the god Attis/Adonis cast, in effigy, out to sea, to be recuperated on the shores of Byblos: or like the good Prince Ferdinand washed ashore after shipwreck and "weeping again the king my father's wrack"; the child Simon, equipped with a rosary of jewels and an earring of gold, will arise from Antipodean waves to be rescued by a Maori Joseph/Hohepa whose savage irascibility will, ironically, replicate the fury of his Celtic progenitor. The impotent anger of a mind debilitated by heroin will be reiterated in the obsessive, alcoholic battering practised by Simon's stepfather Joe. Celtic father and Maori male have both been corrupted by a decadent civilization in which patriarchal authority has completely run amok.

In deconstructing the traditional male hero and reconstructing the heroic stereotype in the figure of a female epic protagonist, Keri Hulme has implemented a strikingly bold and innovative literary project. Kerewin Holmes combines the physical strength and imperturbability of a Hemingway hero with the artistic passion of a Stephen Dedalus and the spiritual perspicacity of Shakespeare's Prospero. Like Joyce's Daedalian artist, she must learn to embrace the compassion and loving commitment exemplified in the emotive life of a disappointed paternal figure, a Maori Leopold/Joe/Hohepa.

Joe complains at one point, that regular work is demeaning because it makes one, in effect, a puppet in someone else's show. (89) Yet Joe and Simon are both so enamoured of Kere that they seem to resemble puppets in her own, somewhat reluctant, domestic drama. "Be wary," she admonishes herself. "Look out for the child . . . but don't let them get too close." (250) Kere may luxuriate in the confidences of a secret soul-book that, like Prospero's tome, signals the magical powers of artistic creation. Once stricken, however, by a mysterious, gut-grinding illness, she lapses into personal and aesthetic impotence. LIke Prospero's players, she must succumb to trials imposed by unfathomable, other-worldly powers. Her own games--emotional, artistic, and relational--have given way to an enigmatic god-game that she completely fails to understand.

Her near-death experience from abdominal cancer, complete with drug-induced, hallucinogenic fantasy, is so meticulously anatomized that her sudden, dream-like recovery seems miraculous indeed. Hulme's narrative always verges on the mysterious and inexplicable world of Maori legend. As in a myth or fairy tale, an ancient, haggard figure of ostensibly indeterminate sex appears out of nowhere and offers a bitter, healing potion to resuscitate the flagging hero. As Kerewin drinks the "sour brew," a "snaggletooth grin" assures longevity to her "lovestrong" nature. (425) At this point, Hulme's romantic tale borders on tribal allegory, embellished, as it is, with a final dream-welcome from Maori ancestors.

Like an Odyssean or Dantesque protagonist, Kerewin makes a trip to the underworld--the night-world of dream and dementia, of hallucination, pain, and physical trauma. With soul steeled through misery and mania, she is resurrected, like the phoenix, to build a circular, womb-like Maori tower that will henceforth provide a home for herself, her soul-mate Joe, and the much-chastened, Christlike Simon.[8] "We can endure anything," Joe proclaims triumphantly. "We are toughened, different, an annealed steel, triple-forged." (444)

Like Joyce in *Ulysses* and *Finnegans Wake*, Keri Hulme employs a self-reflexive, "double spiral" narrative structure.[9] For Simon's own assessment of his figurative death and resurrection, we must return to his fragmented interior monologue, "The End at the Beginning" of *The Bone People*:

> Maybe there is the dance, as she says. Creation and change, destruction and change.
>
> New marae from the old marae, a beginning from the end.
>
> His mind weaves it into a spiral fretted with stars.
>
> He holds out his hand, and it is gently taken. (3)

All three principal characters--Kerewin, Joe, and Simon--have suffered ritual death, purgation, and semi-miraculous resurrection. In the utopian dream of "commensalism" that concludes this allegorical tale, Keri Hulme suggests that New Zealand's future lies neither in Maori separatism nor in Pakeha dominance, but in the celebration of a rich multi-cultural heritage amalgamating the best of Maori, Pakeha and European traditions in a finely-tempered community of human fellowship.

Hulme's Prospero, like her Shakespearean predecessor, ends by destroying the secret soul-book that once empowered her but that, in the comedy of ritual communion and dance, seems no longer necessary. Like James Joyce before her, Hulme celebrates chosen affiliation over familial bonding. And she comes the long way round, through epic narrative, parody, sentimental fiction, and linguistic play, to propose an ethic of love and understanding that might be consigned to the category of romance--but that proves no less compelling in its palimpsestic amalgamation of a Maori dream with European literary tradition. In offering the world a Maori/Pakeha epic, filled with melodrama, coincidence, and carnivalesque play, Keri Hulme has provided a fictional paradigm for the multi-cultural future of New Zealand society.

NOTES

1. In her article entitled "Keri Hulme: Spiralling to Success," Elizabeth Webby suggests that it is possible "to read *The Bone People* allegorically, with Kerewin, Joe and Simon respectively representing the mind, body and spirit which, according to the doctrines of Aikido, once studied by Kerewin in Japan, must be unified if humankind is ever to achieve perfection. But these characters are far from being bloodless abstractions. . . . *The Bone People* offers much more than the cerebral game-playing of much recent fiction--it engages the heart and spirit as well as the mind." [*Meanjin* 44.3 (1985), p. 20]
2. Keri Hulme, *The Bone People* (1984; rpt. New York: Viking Penguin, 1986), p. 4.
3. In "Re-writing their Stories, Renaming Themselves: Post-colonialism and Feminism in the Fictions of Keri Hulme and Audrey Thomas," Chris Prentice notes that Hulme's language "frequently derives from Celtic and Gaelic nuances, and there are particular Joycean influences." [*Span*,

23 (1986), p. 73] "The writing moves between poetry and prose, realism, dream and myth, and the narrative, while generally in the third person, creates, through the strength of Kerewin's consciousness, the impression of first person. . . . The movement between poetry and prose narrative also occurs without clear boundaries."

4. Carmel Gaffney suggests in "Making the Net Whole: Design in Keri Hulme's *The Bone People*" that Hulme has indeed provided us, in the text of her novel, with all the information necessary to untangle Simon's convoluted history; and that it is only the dispersal of red herrings in the fragmented narrative that throws us off a trail of clues that someone like Holmes (Sherlock, that is) could surely trace to a satisfactory conclusion. "The heroin discovered in the wreck links Timon, the Irish heroin addict, with Simon. . . . Hulme simply gives us all the information we need to link Simon with his Irish heroin-addict father; she deliberately evades stressing what should be obvious to us. By making us read attentively Hulme suggests that patterns do exist in life if we have the wit to discern them." [*Southerly,* 46 (1986), p. 300] Susan Ash, in her article "*The Bone People* after *Te Kaihau*," does not comment on "A Drift in Dream" as the novel's "pre-text." [*World Literature Written in English,* 29.1 (1989), pp. 123-35) I am grateful to Professor Elizabeth Webby, of Sydney University, for calling my attention to Hulme's fascinating intertextuality.

5. In his book *In Palamedes' Shadow*, Robert Rawdon Wilson explains that a "godgame signifies a gamelike situation in which a *magister ludi* knows the rules (because he has invented them) and the character-player does notice. A godgame occurs in literature when one or more characters creates an illusion, a mazelike sequence of false accounts, that entraps other characters. . . . The master of the game is godlike in that he exercises powers, holds an advantageous position, will probably be beyond detection, . . . and may even be, like Oberon or Ariel in Shakespeare's plays, invisible." [Boston: Northeastern University Press, 1990, pp. 123-24] In *The Tempest*: "Prospero's godgame variously reveals the natures of his shipwrecked countrymen and, as well, he imposes a judgement upon them." (p. 129)

6. Keri Hulme, *Te Kaihau/The Windeater* (1986; rpt. London: Hodder and Stoughton, 1987), p. 193. Hereafter cited in the text as *TK*.
7. In the tradition of recent French feminist criticism, I have deliberately set up a French/English pun in the hyphenated neologisms of this sentence.
8. In her article "*the bone people:* (Not) Having It Both Ways," Judith Dale interprets Simon as a Christ-figure, "an emblem of vicarious expiation for the loss, brokenness and guilt the other two were suffering from." [*Landfall,* 39 (1985), pp. 419-20] "Simon's way," she concludes, is "the way of the cross, and for this reason his tragic presence in the book richly counterbalances the comedic finale. (p. 321) In a note, Dale shares a personal communication from Keri Hulme objecting to the comparison of Simon with Christ and identifying "his 'provenance' as 'the Celtic "marvellous stranger" or "marvellous child" (Aifa and Cuchulain's son Connla, or Arianrhod's child Dylan, from the *Mabinogion*).'" (pp. 427-28) Dale, however, holds her critical ground and, in her final assessment of the text, observes that the "novel wants, needs, to have it both ways . . . so that we are able to see Kerewin . . . as independent, self-sufficient, and androgynous: . . . she both is and is not to be united with Joe." (pp. 426-27)
9. Elizabeth Webby comments that the structure of *The Bone People* simulates "that of the double spiral, where beginning and ending are in perpetual interchange. . . . The double spiral is also a traditional Maori symbol, and fundamental to the novel is the idea that change and renewal do not mean a total rejection of the past." (pp. 17-19)

Fantasy and Flight in the Novels of Maurice Gee

SOM PRAKASH

One of the three dominant images Roger Robinson identifies in Gee's novels is the pattern of a reclusive, bookish figure retreating into the security of "intellectual and moralistic abstraction" in order to avoid the practical demands of family life.[1] But books and abstract ideas are not the only means of escape. While Arthur Pinnock or George Plumb can retreat into their life of the mind, their wives can find refuge in their gentility. Obsessions are as likely to be a cause as they are a means of retreat, and there are many characters in Gee who are obsessed with one thing or another--Oliver Plumb and Wendy Philson, Merle Butters and her husband, Donny Andrews and his father, and so on. Kingsley finds introspection, amongst other things, a helpful instrument to veil the truth about his family from himself. Sometimes the truth the characters are consciously or unconsciously avoiding might be too hurtful or unmanageable if brought out into the open. Or it might be an external sign of an inner condition that a character decides is best not faced; for example, Plumb finds the eels repulsive with their intimations of evil, while Paul Prior's disgust with the deterioration and pollution around him is at least partly a displaced response to potential corruption that he knows lies within him, and certainly within his brother.

Part of Ray's problems, not to mention his ambivalent relationship with Duggie, can be explained in the same way. Ray is often aware that his cleverness, like Kingsley's wit and imagination, forms part of his tactical evasion of reality. If Ray's indulgence in second-rate journalism helps him to avoid more worthwhile or demanding writing as long as possible, Kingsley's walls covered with maps--and especially his lurid map of his marriage, cynically entitled "Partnership Island"--show just how badly he wants to avoid the bitter truth. As an additional measure, Kingsley comforts himself by imagining flattering futures for his children or by translating his grubby father into such literary or romantic figures as Tom Brangwen or Arawata Bill. It is instructive that the father and the son envy each other's position, each engaged in his own form of evasion. Finally, there seems to be a common underlying reason for these forms of flight and fantasy. Characters like Ray, Kingsley and Paul become aware, at least occasionally, that their tendency to avoid reality springs from their lack of substance or centre. It is a sense of the void within themselves which they find rather unsettling, which in turn leads to further evasion.

The Literary Recluse

Even if Maurice Gee doesn't know exactly why the literary recluse is such a common figure in his novels, the ambivalence attached to retreating into a world of books and ideas is hardly in doubt.[2] As we see in *In My Father's Den*, an enclosed library of books can be both a place of refuge and a means of avoiding reality and responsibility, a storehouse for knowledge as well as poison. If Paul's boyhood was spent in a prison "watched over by his mother," the den "turns out, ironically, to be a place of family bondage for an adult as well."[3] On the other hand, Charlie Inverarity's contempt for books contrasts unfavourably with his daughter Celia's love for them, although his criticism of Paul as an "arty bloke" seems to have some validity. Charlie regards books as "muck" which "never got anyone anywhere." "He is right, it never did, alone," says Williamson, reminding us that in New Zealand fiction, books and arty blokes are constantly derided by philistines like Charlie.[4] George Plumb's own attachment to books makes him believe that others, especially his children, also see his study as "Alladin's cave"; but in *Meg* we discover that the children tend to see it not so much as a magic cave but as a prison, a place for punishment and retribution.

In contrast to Plumb's magical world of books, the fifteen acres of Peacehaven become Robert's magic land. It is implied that through his proximity to nature, Robert is able to heal

Plumb's bee-sting or burnt hand, even Betty's retarded mind. Equally magically, he manages to communicate words to his father "almost independent of sound."[5] It is ironical that the brilliant father should learn the true meaning of love from this simple son. For Plumb, books are often a convenient means of escape from reality--and he is not always unaware of this, as we have seen. After Robert's trial for refusing to join the army, Meg leaves "Dad in the city browsing in bookshops. He would read heavily to cure his disappointment." (*M*, 152) Part of this disappointment is that Plumb's eloquent sixteen-page statement for the Tribunal (speaking of the "necessity of a New Way of Love beyond the old religions" against "the pagan barbarities of the imperialistic war") remains in Robert's pocket, unread and wasted.[6] If obsession with books and ideas is a means of escape from reality, it also blinds Plumb to reality. The day after his visit to Robert in detention, he sends "a parcel of books" to the son who is least interested in reading and who "asked nothing about Peacehaven but Dad did not seem to notice." (*M*, 159) Moreover, he mistakenly thinks Robert is doing well in detention. Both Plumb's blind--and blinding--attitude towards books or learning and Maurice Gee's ambivalence towards them are neatly captured in the episode where Meg packs Robert's books in preparation for his move to the cottage:

> The books had been Dad's. His own were there: *The Growing Point of Truth, New Reasons for the Future Life, The World's Disease.* He was good at titles. And each had its tag of Latin, boldly pencilled at poor Robert: *Post tenebras lux* and *Tempori parendum.* They confused me too. I wanted to cry, "Onward!"; yet was saying, "Enough of this stuff, Dad, enough!" I closed the books roughly, packed them in.
>
> "Do you ever read these, Robert?"
>
> "I'm not much of a reader." He pushed himself up painfully from the table. "I never really knew what he was getting at." (*M*, 54)

Meg's own ambivalence can be explained in terms of the multiple role books have played in her life. On one hand, they have rescued her from threats and despair; on the other, they have been responsible for her romantic view of life.[7] A major portion of her early acceptance of adversity is based on fantasy rather than reality. Her father's actual prison, for instance, appears just *ordinary* to Meg, unlike the prison of her reading and imagination, which is stone-walled and towered, temporarily preventing a heroic father from putting the world to rights. With hindsight, she is able to laugh at the effect her romantic reading has produced in her: "I thought of myself as possessing (and wrote it too) a gently welling cup to happiness. The books I read and the language they taught me!" The books she reads, however, also compensate for the tragedy that surrounds her family, enabling her to cry "out with belief" at times. Thus the questions that interest Gee with regard to books are quite complex, as Bill Manhire has correctly observed. Meg's romantic novels can obscure vision as much as her father's "worthier" texts. Is Felicity right in suggesting that print and solitude are drugs her father is hooked on? Are people more important than books? Perhaps Plumb realizes this at the end, but does Paul Prior? Many of Gee's most interesting characters are caught somewhere between people and books, being tugged in both directions. The reservations which Gee's novels express about books are based on an assumption about their intrinsic value, says Manhire: "George Plumb in his study is also a heroic figure engaged on an intellectual adventure. Whatever we think of him, we do not prefer the materialist work ethic of Cheeseman and Hay."[8]

Ideas and Obsessions

Plumb's intellectual adventure would be altogether laudable if it weren't for his almost total "retreat from the quotation," as pedantic Oliver puts it. While Meg also sees the father escaping into Browning or Emerson when family gets too much for him, she tries to see him from her mother's point of view. Edie clearly understood that the "Quotidian" was her part of the contract: "His was to seek after truth, to stand and fight. He martyred himself to his conscience, and she to him. She of course had a better understanding of it all." So there is some justification for Plumb's behaviour. What is unforgivable in him, however, is the lack of love or humanity that results from his retreat. Obviously, Felicity overstates her case, but she is basically right in suggesting that in his study with his books he was "making one little room an everywhere--but, poor old thing, in human terms he was nowhere." With Plumb's grand notions about humanity, there is bound to be a serious disjunction between his belief and actual practice. Apart from his patently cruel treatment of his homosexual son, Plumb is at least as often right as he is wrong. As grave as they are, Plumb's weaknesses are finally seen to be not only human but also curable.

This is not always true for other characters who entertain grand notions about human destiny. Wendy has great strengths but equally great weaknesses. When the real world becomes too difficult for her she pastes paper over it and creates an unreal one in order to survive. Since she believes in Plumb in an unrealistic way, she nearly loses her reason, not to mention her life, when she is disillusioned by his imperfections. Unable to function fully in this life, she has intimations of a world beyond. The fabulous peak she climbs towards is at once the cause and the symptom of her misplaced faith, industry and cleverness, which together lead her further and further away from reality. Meg hopes that George Plumb Wendy is so busy creating will keep her satisfied: "If he failed her it would be the failure of the main prop of her world. But I had little fear for her. She had great cunning and strength of mind." Her spiritual quests are exactly the opposite of Plumb's or Meg's attempts to come to grips with the present reality of their human lives. Her interest in Jung's interpretation of dreams like her belief in reincarnation, enables her to dream her other lives. That her indulgent search, on the whole, overlooks the human factor is recognized by Raymond, who foresees her fossicking in the burnt cottage and coming upon the Buddha as a treasure, crowning her precious acquisition; however, what is everything for Wendy is nothing to Ray--Peacehaven without the Plumbs. In other words, ideas seem to matter more to Wendy than people. Even so, for all her weaknesses, Wendy is in earnest, unlike the intellectual butterflies that Merle and Graydon are.[9] Their escape from reality takes the form of flitting from movement to movement, the glass wall of their money providing them with security they hardly need. Plumb is both fascinated and repelled by them, perhaps because he sees a part of himself in them.[10]

Another signal of escapism in Maurice Gee's work is materialism. In his implied value scheme, an undue emphasis on, or succumbing to, materialistic values is often a symptom of insensitivity to the reality of other people. Fred Meggett, Fergus Sole, or Duggie Plumb, buoyed by obsessions of one form or another, sometimes forget their own real limitations. Oliver approves of Emerson not only because of the latter's success in pioneering and commercial aviation but also because "Emerson had made money." Given the type of people they are, their mutual admiration is predictable. Oliver in his high judicial role, or with his superior sense of morality, is as removed from reality as Emerson in his aerial seclusion or in his successful tomato-growing venture. The truly adventurous spirit which characterizes the Sundowner of the skies disappears with his glass metropolis, which is so "far from nature" that Robert's physical or mental condition can hardly endure it. His house, likewise, is affluent and stylish, but the lounge remains unlived, and unlivable. His new life-style is a virtual betrayal of his earlier adventurous spirit, a betrayal which is as inexplicable as his eleventh-hour cancellation of the book on his famous aerial feats. If Raymond's literary dream is dashed, it is Gee's even-handed manner of demonstrating that flights of fancy, for the uncle as well as the nephew, have a way of ending in disappointment.

Threats and Retreats

Some characters find themselves fleeing from reality when it becomes too threatening for them in one way or another. Just as Paul's father, in his struggles for privacy from his sister and his wife, finds the den a safe but ambivalent refuge, Paul uses the den to save himself from his mother's grimly fundamental Presbyterianism.[11] As a cave dweller, he feels safe from the tangle of ghastly events, or their moral implications. Almost all members of the Pinnock family show the same tendency to retreat; Arthur withdraws from his family into his life of the mind; the mother, who retreats into a world of "gentility" that excludes all vivacity or coarseness of life, ensures her children too can feel comfortable only when life is remote.[12]

As a child, Meg runs home to the clean, secure world of her mother's kitchen when threatened by confusing, adult behaviour. Esther's cool, almost contemptuous acceptance of her ugliness that results from her careless greed for comforts--like her later acceptance of Fred calling her Fatso, Guzzleguts, Pisshead--appears at first glance a head-on collision with reality, but in fact it is also a form of flight. If as an adolescent she goes "too far, too carelessly," as an adult Esther talks "all racehorses and poker schools." But since her "winnings gave her happiness only briefly," she soon "looked on them as a dirty trick--and lost soon enough." This is Meg's view of her elder sister. For her own part, Meg manages to turn some of her flights from reality to her advantage. Her romantic reading providing her with the resources to cope with not only the failures of her sister but also the need for romance and success in her own life.

Her reading is but one of a combination of means Meg uses to combat the threats in her life; nostalgia, dreams, violence, even work or service are others. When the birth of her first child makes her realize that everything has happened too fast, "that there were things I should have known, and should have done, before I married," she thinks again of the Black River and the Land of the missing, yearning for Peacehaven and the Plumbs, and sometimes for the world, "which came before my eyes in story-book shapes and story-book colours." (*M,* 116) To see the world in its ordinary shapes and forms is too threatening a proposition for her to accept serenely. It could mean, for example, the ugly reality of her husband's toothless face that results from sheer stupidity and greed; the violence that Meg displays in such a case is as much a form of flight as the impossible desire to return to Mother, to the safe, fantastic world of childhood and nostalgia. After the death of her mother, Meg's flights take her to Robert, or his cottage, where she feels safer and more useful, away from her painful family or marital problems. Robert's death gives her the strength to accept the pain of existence and virtually removes the need for further evasions.

Unfortunately, not everyone has the luxury of Meg's solution. Esther, for example, succumbs increasingly to alcohol in order to avoid facing the painful futility of her life, while Alfred is unable to rise above his hatred and frustrations and virtually drinks himself to death. As his inability to get a rose from his mother's garden, or to re-enter the world that has rejected him demonstrate, the past cannot always be re-created nostalgically in order to rectify a bitter present. Meg roots out Mother's rose garden after Father's death because it requires too much work. Moreover, "in moving in hat and glove among her roses Mother was playing the lady she might have been," which strikes Meg as a falsification. Even so, Meg understands her mother's need of her only pretence. Flights into a reassuring past are often necessary even though they might appear self-destructive in some regards. With a deft touch, Gee links the children's need to escape with that of the parents's, as if to imply a cause-effect relationship. After banishing Alfred, Plumb gives up bodily cleanliness for a while, a sign to Meg of an inner coldness. Meg watches her parents fighting that coldness by mutual kindness, slowly puzzling out their way to happiness, doing their round of the garden but keeping clear of the orchard: "It was unreal. I sat at my books in the evenings and heard their laughter coming from the study. It was unreal. It was our new reality." (*M*, 102)

The new reality that people create is especially important in times of crisis. At Alfred's funeral, a tearful Willis speaks about Alfred as a boy, inventing a good deal, but he seems to believe his own invention.[13] At least as far as Meg is concerned, Willis's story serves no less a useful purpose than the incongruous funeral service itself. Meg understands the need for some people to avoid what is real or true, to promote an image that is flattering or totally unrealistic. As Manhire shows, one of the roles films play in Gee's early fiction is to supply "stylized models of 'real life' which provincial and adolescent New Zealand might aspire to."[14] A 46-year-old man can live "for two hours with guns in his hands." In young Meg's case, the need for security, given her vulnerable universe, becomes so important that she is determined to ignore the facts in favour of her belief in the sackman.

In *Games of Choice*, the title itself implies both the games of choice and the games of chance the characters are caught up in. As Manhire says, people "not only play the games but also write the rules they will play by, choosing the lives they lead even as they remain persuaded that those lives have simply happened to them." Even passiveness "involves co-operation with circumstance." On the other hand, there are the games of fantasy which enable them "to imagine, along with agreeable futures, the lives they might have led."[15] Thus Kingsley "used every trick he knew to keep himself from a backward glance at life. That could only lead to the game of choices, to the dreaming of other ways, which spread him thin."[16] Despite this reluctance, he cannot help drifting into the past at times, in order to "remember and manage events," especially in the company of a father who "was inventing too, though he no longer knew it." Kingsley, however, is more self-conscious; he can recall his mother thirty years after her death and fashion

> a boyhood to please her, in which his gentleness matched hers and his savagery was against "bad men" and his understanding and care prolonged her life. Later he considered himself with dislike: he had a shallow tricky mind. (*GC*, 23-24)

As Kingsley seems aware, if fashioning a past as a means of evading the present is a dangerous activity, rejecting that past altogether is tantamount to a rejection of the self. Unlike George Plumb, or Meg for that matter, Kingsley does not regard the processes of memory as entirely positive, let alone religious.

Bruised beyond all endurance, Robert rejects his father's offer of the cottage in favour of Parminter's farm; for Robert Peacehaven is part of the world, a world that has hurt him. As the father recognizes, "The world in a way was hell; and this place, the Ark, stood outside it. Parminter's craziness was necessary to Robert."[17] In fact, while Robert finds useful work and does it well, which is a means of retaining his sanity, he has no more illusions about Parminter than he has about his own healing powers. His form of flight from the world is seen, then, to be necessary, if not also healthy, although Gee, through Raymond, raises some important questions about it. What is not in doubt is Gee's compassion. He understands perfectly well the reasons behind Robert's flight. Even Parminter's fantastic world, which borders dangerously on delusion, is treated with compassion and understanding, if also with irony and wry humour. So what we see in Maurice Gee's work as a whole is that often there is a salutary ambivalence attached to the various kinds of flights from reality. After all, a re-examination of the past, as in the case of the narrators of the trilogy, may be seen as a flight from too overwhelming a present. But a realistic review of that present in terms of its correct relationship with the past leads to an accurate understanding of the self--and hopefully to a meaningful acceptance of it.

NOTES

1. The other two images are: the process of observation, and in particular secret, voyeuristic observation of the world from a secure vantage point; and "the apparent inarticulateness even of fulfilled self-knowledge." Roger Robinson, "New Zealand," unpublished essay, 1989, soon to be published in a book entitled *The Commonwealth Novel Since 1960* (Macmillan), ed. Bruce King.
2. Regarding the literary recluse, Gee is reported as saying: "He keeps getting in. I'm not sure what it means." David Hill, *Introducing Maurice Gee* (Auckland: Longman Paul, 1981), p 53.
3. Donald Hannah, "Family Chronicles: The Novels of Maurice Gee," *Kunapipi,* III, 2 (1981), p. 85.
4. Jim Williamson, "The Potent Beast," Rev. of *In My Father's Den* by Gee, *Islands,* 1,1 (1972), p. 75.
5. Of course, the fact that books also communicate meaning "almost independent of sound" is especially important to someone like Plumb who is deaf. He believes, though, "By deafness you can hear the inaudible, see the invisible and touch the incomprehensible." *Meg* (London: Faber, 1981), p. 137.
6. History repeats itself with a vengeance: Plumb himself was unable to read his equally eloquent statement during his own trial.
7. As a child she identifies the seven Plumbs together with the seven Australians of the book, Judy's final sacrifice reflecting Meg's desire to preserve the Plumb family.
8. Bill Manhire, *Maurice Gee*. (Auckland: Oxford UP, 1986), p. 68.
9. Wendy is also generous; she accommodates Merle at Peacehaven to save her from going into a home. Merle, for her part, will leave all her money to the Spiritualist Church. She even begrudges paying for the electricity she uses.
10. Their fear of intellectual interference with their child's

natural responses is an oblique if humorous reminder that Plumb's intellectualizing has interfered with his own as well as others's growth and understanding.

11. Donald Hannah, pp. 83-84.
12. Brian Boyd, "Maurice Gee: Ironies of Growth and Judgement," *Islands,* 83 (1980), pp. 269-70.
13. Willis was away at sea for most of Alfred's childhood. His selective and inventive memory also seems to operate regarding his ninety-six women, some of whom he claims he has paid for, although Alfred thinks he takes his numbers seriously.
14. Bill Manhire, p. 14.
15. *Ibid.*, p. 28.
16. Maurice Gee, *Games of Choice* (1976; Wellington: Oxford UP, 1977), p. 16.
17. Maurice Gee, *Plumb*. (London: Faber, 1978), p. 190.

New Zealand Poetry: What's New, What's Comtemporary?

LAWRENCE BOURKE

Is there no progress in art? Harvey McQueen and Ian Wedde, who edited *The Penguin Book of New Zealand Verse* of 1985, and suffered the consequences,[1] went on to edit *The Penguin Book of Contemporary New Zealand Poetry. Nga Kupu Titohu o Aotearoa.*[2] Taking up where the previous anthology left off, the new anthology moves squarely into the world where reputations and egos are very much alive and kicking to become even more contentious.

The Australian poet John Forbes exclaimed that few other English speaking countries could at present offer so strong and varied a collection as *The Penguin Book of Contemporary New Zealand Poetry*. Perhaps the forthcoming 1992 Penguin collection of contemporary Australian poetry may change his mind. But certainly in its range no less than its heights the new McQueen and Wedde anthology is witness to the liveliness of contemporary New Zealand poetry. We expect strong work from writers who have been publishing since at least the sixties, and find it here; and so too with those who began publishing in the seventies: Murray Edmond, Cilla McQueen, Elizabeth Smither, Ian Wedde. Where the anthology can surprise is with its selection from writers who began publishing in the eighties: Janet Charman, John Dickson, Kim Eggleton, David Eggleton, Anne French, Dinah Hawken, Michele Leggott, Graham Lindsay, Elizabeth Nannestad, John Newton, Gregory O'Brien and Fiona Farrell Poole. Just the length of the roll call indicates the richness of the period. If it is a New Zealand landmark the new Penguin is also, appropriately, an active one.

An anthology like this is, however, more than a collection of poems. Both in its selection and Introduction it becomes a cultural marker, whether by its advancement, entrenchment or revision of a set of values. The new Penguin anthology plainly declares its stand for variety and egalitarianism. With just under 500 pages of verse and over fifty English language poets, the anthology seems to celebrate democratic pluralism, the doors opening for all kinds of writers. There is a massive infusion of writers, in fact some 29--or just over half--of the poets writing in English in the new book are not in the 1985 Penguin.

Certainly the 1989 Penguin is the most comprehensive of the recent anthologies of contemporary New Zealand poetry, of which there have been four: Murray Edmond and Mary Paul's *The New Poets of the 80's: Initiatives in New Zealand Poetry*, Louis Johnson's miscellany *Antipodes New Writing*, Mark Williams's *The Caxton Press Anthology: New Zealand Poetry 1972-1986* and Lydia Wevers's *Yellow Pencils: Contemporary Poetry by New Zealand Women*.[3] As the subtitles indicate, *New Poets* and *Yellow Pencils* have a specialist focus. Rather than offering a markedly different map of New Zealand poetry, the new Penguin tends to go over the same ground these anthologies travelled separately and brings the various elements together. Readers will still turn to *New Poets* and *Yellow Pencils* for their more exclusive concerns as well as for their editor's discussion of the selections. Unlike these anthologies and *The Caxton Press Anthology* with Mark Williams's essay on contemporary New Zealand poetry, the new Penguin offers little in the way of editorial overview or comment on its selection.

While the new anthology will not displace these other works it does collect eight writers previously unpresented in the main New Zealand poetry anthologies. Eric Beach and Nigel Roberts who have both lived in Australia since the early seventies offer strong poems. Beach was represented in Arthur Baysting's *The Young New Zealand Poets* (1973); to the best of my knowledge, Roberts is collected for the first time in a New Zealand anthology. Rob Allan, whose assured poetry has so far appeared only in periodicals and in *Antipodes New Writing*, is another "new" writer represented by lively poems.

The broadening of the catchment suggests an editorial commitment to the democratization of poetry. Harvey McQueen declares:

> Obviously major established writers who had been productive throughout the decade would be represented generously, as would certain mid-career writers and significant new writers. But we did make a conscious decision very early on to be as non-hierarchical as possible. (16)

In the 1985 Introduction, Ian Wedde wrote of the intention to recover the demotic and move away from the hieratic. McQueen's "conscious decision" to be "non-hierarchical" seems to be part of that trend, which aligns the anthology with a compelling movement in modern poetry.

Edmond and Paul in *New Poets* place the subversion of hierarchy in poetry within a general context. There is a lost consensus, they argue, of what poetry is and who defines it. From "celebrating the disparate," they turn to those who respond "less positively" to these "developments" and happily call forth the bogey of C.K. Stead. Stead--with his terms "excellence" and "talent"--is soon dispatched and wiping their hands of that business the enlightened editors quote "there is no such thing as talent, only its manifest lack." (x) (I would have thought that to say "here is the manifest lack of something" necessitated the existence of that thing somewhere else?) Presumably the editors chose not to print everything that came before them. Their selection, whether theorized or not, reflects a notion of standards, of "excellence." While they happily dismiss one set of standards, when it comes to disclosing their own they fall back onto gestures and "personal choice," which suggests a mysticism of a superior sensibility.

In his introduction Harvey McQueen genuflects in the familiar way to the post-modernist sensibility, but says little about his and his co-editor's selection. He remarks that "it is too soon to pin a theory, or theories, to what is happening in New Zealand verse, except to note that there is a lot happening." (16) But not all poets in New Zealand are included in the new Penguin--the absences are made more surprising by the seeming inclusiveness. The Keatsian appeal of that refusal "to pin a theory" covers a choice to be silent over what it is that McQueen believes "is happening" as much as a refusal to declare a prior allegiance to standards, however they are articulated.

Despite "numbers" being an old synonym for verses, poetry

is notoriously a matter of quality rather than quantity. All the same, statistics do have their uses. We might count heads within the new Penguin, for instance, and argue that the numbers reflect a dismissal of "elitist notions of excellence" in poetry. And we might go on to present this as evidence of egalitarianism either in the editors or more widely in New Zealand. It is nevertheless worth recalling that W.F. Alexander and A.E. Currie in their 1906 anthology *New Zealand Verse* collected 55 poets and 174 poems--which is not greatly different from the new Penguin's 58 or so poets writing in English and 240 poems.

Opening their anthology Alexander and Currie announced that what they were representing was "minor poetry." How many of those in the new Penguin fit the same category? But it is that very "minor" and "major" division which the new Penguin raises for contention. That is, the anthology, like most interesting anthologies, reflects a thesis. Whether the thesis reflects an escape from elitism or a submission to mediocrity is, I would think, worth exploring. Given the stakes, it is a pity that McQueen does not address the issues raised by his anthology.

It is said that contemporary New Zealand poetry is too diverse to support generalizations beyond that generalization--which is hard to quarrel with after reading the new *Penguin*. The poetry varies in mode from representational to surreal, with subjects ranging from the country to the city, and is written by poets ranging from those who began publishing in the thirties through to those who began publishing in the eighties. But diversity does not necessarily invalidate the use of notions such as "excellence" or "talent." By collecting such a range of poets, the anthology gives an opportunity to ask whether there might be shared terms for discussion and evaluation, even if these terms do little more or less than help clarify personal likes and dislikes. This is another reason why it is a pity that the editors made no comment on their selection.

McQueen does highlight the prominence of the long poem in the anthology, which he argues redresses a previous imbalance, an emphasis upon the lyric. He points out that the long poem seems to be popular among contemporary New Zealand poets and should be represented. (16) But again there is no guide to what this might mean. Does the popularity reflect interest in contemporary North American poets like Robert McDowell who work in the "new narrative"? Or maybe the popularity is appropriate from the country which gave the world the long poem to end all long poems, Alfred Domett's *Ranolf and Amohia*, even if that work should have elicited from Tennyson, himself no slouch at the long poem, the droll irony that Domett "but wants limitation to be a very considerable poet"?

What else beside the long poem does the anthology promote? The new *Penguin*, like its forerunner, is proudly bi-lingual. In 1985 McQueen and Wedde were criticized for selecting poems in a language neither knew, now they restrict themselves to the English language section while Miriama Evans looks after the Maori poetry. Of all the pages available for poetry, the Maori language poets have about 16% of the total--which as it happens reflects the current New Zealand demographic mix. The rough average of 3 pages per Maori language poet is in fact rather less because these pages include both original texts and their translations.

58 English language poets occupy the remaining 420 pages, which offers an average of just over 7 pages per poet. In practice few poets are allotted the average. Their placement constitutes a hierarchy, not as peaked as in previous anthologies but nevertheless a ranking which sorts the new writers. Distribution tends toward three categories: those poets who get rather more than average; those a little less than average; and those with noticeably less. Familiar names occupy the highest rung. Allen Curnow gets twenty pages. The others are Lauris Edmond (12 pages), Murray Edmond (12), Bill Manhire (11), Vincent O'Sullivan (12), Kendrick Smithyman (13), C.K. Stead (12), and Ian Wedde (11). The surprise, for me at least, is Alistair Campbell whose selection runs to 15 pages.

The newer poets are relegated to the lower decks. The highest of these "junior" levels is around five pages, the lowest around three. Some of these writers have yet to establish a body of work but this is not always the case. Some new poets however do receive the nod. Dinah Hawken whose *It Has No Sound And Is Blue* (1987) won "Best First Book" award in the 1987 Commonwealth Poetry Prize has 11 pages. But clearly the editors's pick for canonization is Michele Leggott at 14 pages.

Michele Leggott's long poem "An Island" is taken in its entirety and printed sideways to accommodate its exploded margins. "An Island" has all the hallmarks of becoming a reference point in New Zealand poetry. It is a *tour de force* in developing imagistic moments into a long work. It also stands out for its exploitation of margins--which, I assume, are to represent the great spaces and light of the Pacific Ocean, and to evoke a new sense of time, an expansive ocean rhythm which measures life on the Pacific. For all this, the poem irritates me; I find the typographical layout contrived, and I am put off by the elegant obliquity of that assured North American voice ("the world turned some more") with its assumption that it can colonize so many different Pacific voices.

Hierarchy in any selection is probably inevitable, and it may be good, but rather than argue the case for it, the editors implied that they were out to discredit such elitist notions. The silence calls attention to their claim to have made a "conscious decision . . . to be non-hierarchical" and to how they slip past that position with the phrase "as possible," which raises the question of why the editors felt they must take up the position at all? What the grading reflects, beyond senior and junior school, is a preference for certain kinds of poetry.

McQueen also draws attention to the big subject of Wedde's Introduction: language. The issue, we learn, is not just any attitude toward or use of language but taking "language as a tool for research and something active in itself rather than as, primarily, a means of expression," (17) which as I understand it is to oppose self-referentiality and mimeticism. The technique of this opposition is by now a familiar strategy to discredit "realism" and is no more convincing for being so well worn.

Not all the writers in the new Penguin are determined to deconstruct, nor does this necessarily mean that they subscribe to a naive mimeticism, as if any really interesting writer does. One writer who seemingly works in a representational and expressive mode is Anne French, who had two poetry books published when this anthology came out, *All Cretans Are Liars* which won the 1988 New Zealand Book Award for Poetry, and *The Male As Evader*.[4] Clearly she is a proven writer in terms of quality and productiveness. Yet at three pages she is one of the least represented English language writers.

Why is French so narrowly represented? A comparison with more favoured new writers suggests that the reason concerns form and mimeticism. French mostly works with around a dozen lines in language characterized by referentiality, epigrammatic concision and clarity. She is not naive about representation as a hostile reader might claim, but nor does she abandon intentionality and claims about a social reality, an occasion which language evades, colours or refers to but which is not enclosed in language itself, like the kite in her poem of that name:

> It is a live thing, tugging
> at the end of its lines. It is not docile. (186)

An editorial preference for linguistic and formal experimentalism disadvantages those who continue to work with referentiality, and particularly those who continue to find use for clarity and directness. Once again, there may be a good argument for a preference to become an aesthetic criterion, but one would like to hear the argument. Certainly until the case is put it looks like academic fashion dictating, and post-Saussurean self-reference becomes the one value whose significance is never questioned.

The opposition between "expressive realism" and non-representational "experimentalism" is misleading and unproductive. One can see this from the work of the new writers as much as from the established figures. Writers continue to use representation and in their use recognize that it is not unproblematic.

Fiona Farrell Poole in the "Passenger" songs adapts the nineteenth-century folk song or broadsheet ballad of the kind that circulated around the streets of London and Liverpool and which reflected and informed the lives of the poorer emigrants. Poole gives the bare "artless" sing-song rhythms of the broadsheet ballads an immediate reference, and uses them in soliloquies rather like the novelist's technique of free and indirect discourse. The forms become emblematic of the character, of her senstimentality, or, as with Charlotte O'Neil, of her directness and resolve. (Here I would like to quote, but the poem, like the ballads, working through repetition and accretion cannot be properly represented through extracts.) "Charlotte O'Neil's Song" in its dramatization of a strong female character about to sail from England offers an historical portrait of the will for economic and political egalitarianism. It is also an ironic comment on the contemporary context. A more obvious writer might have lamented how the ninetenth-century reform ideals which informed much emigration to New Zealand have been derailed by the resurgence of nineteenth-century economic "rationalism" in the contemporary scene. Poole, more subtly, invites us through her selection of form and subject to find the ironies for ourselves.

John Newton's landscape poems in their very different way also seem to be "artless." Newton's poems are refined to the point where the art is to convince that there is no art. Reworking a Romantic nature lyricism he depicts encounters with New Zealand landscape in a way reminiscent of Baxter but perhaps more so of the first section of Fairburn's "Elements." The freshness of observation in Newton's poems returns us to a particular time and place, while like the adzes unearthed in his poem "National Grid" the poems also and without any sense of contrivance call up a past. The three poems by which he is represented converge on a secular epiphanic moment. In "National Grid" it is an ironic epiphany--the speaker recalls when he used to stand beneath a newly built pylon:

> Days when the wind blew spray off the sea
> you could hear the insulators
>
> buzzing in the salt and wet
> Thistles grew back in the bulldozer tracks
> while under the wires
> the static
> stood your hair on end. (358)

There is a cinematic, almost a photo-realist, purity and starkness, to these lines; things and actions seem to exist unmediated, unencumbered by description and qualification. As the careful sound patterning indicates, however, the effect of transparency is just that, an effect, prepared and shaped. In these poems little is claimed for the experience. Newton declares his contemporaneity not by any kind of linguistic self-reference, but by the refusal to extrapolate or universalize. Setting out the private experience, he places it in a social context, as in the lines above with their unstated but unmistakable comment on environmental and social degradation. The national "grid," we come to see, is not entirely metaphoric. An opposition of realism or experimentalism is beside the point in talking of these poems; they exhibit both. Unlike French's poems, however, Newton's avoid traditional-looking metres and stanzas enough to pass for post-modernist.

John Dickson also re-visits Romanticism, but with a greater interest in social groups viewed from one specific aspect: New Zealand's masculinist frontier myth of the good keen man. In a section from "The Empire's Last Drunk" the speaker, a kind of Persian traveller reporting from the outside, considers some locals, one in particular:

> every time he spoke
> he said 'fucking oath' so often
> I assumed he was invoking a tribal god;
> yet later when he talked of how he set crayfish pots
> two miles from land
> he didn't once use those words.
> He also said
> I cannot swim. Death by drowning
> is as good
> as any. (141-42)

For the first part of this narrative comment seems extraneous--except maybe to grunt "strewth," which seems to be one of Dickson's points, how reductive that particular discourse can be. As the narrative unfolds we learn how the important things exist outside the culture's licensed "oath" to its "tribal god."

These poets are not concerned with an authorizing self which sings itself through an "original" rhetoric. Nor with language itself. They are highly alert to the connections between discourse and identity, representation and reality. It is not the gee-whizzeries of "I fall upon the thorns of life" or "all the world's a fiction" which interests them, but the meeting-place where the culture impinges upon and disables or enables experience.

All the same, McQueen's comment about "language" might help us consider what if anything besides printer's glue holds these poems together in the one anthology. A more productive exploration of the language-question I think would leave the dead-end of representation-or-experimentalism to investigate the use of vernacular idioms in an art form with its "elitist" traditions--elitist in that any complex occupation involves specialists who do their craft better than others.

Any anthology will have its key organizing term which no doubt in most cases will be problematic. In the past the term has been national, as in how to define "New Zealand" when collecting "New Zealand" poetry. For McQueen and Wedde national identity is no longer so urgent, hence they freely recover the work of long-term expatriates. For them the awkward term is "contemporary." For McQueen it means up to the mark, "now," "post-Baxter." For Miriama Evans editing the Maori section it involves:

> a cultural perception of time and the indivisibility of past, present and future into discrete segments. Thus a holistic recognition of "contemporary" is not just confined to the "here and now" but is enmeshed with the traditional and futuristic. (19-20)

Evans includes work over a hundred years old, because it "remains pertinent . . . and continues to inspire." (20) The honorifics with which she surrounds her interpretation of "contemporary" implicitly work against McQueen's use of the term. An editor may find that an earlier New Zealand poem written in English remains generative, but an anthology of "contemporary" poetry is generally understood to mean giving space to living writers, which precludes reprinting much earlier work. What might be behind Evans's statement is a need to make early Maori texts readily available whereas those written and already published in English are for the most part in print. Perhaps it would be better to have a comprehensive anthology of Maori poetry, rather than forcing it between the bindings with another poetry particularly when it is done with an emphasis upon difference, as happens here with the interpretations of the key organizing term "contemporary." Such an emphasis upon difference encourages simplistic--and, surely?--dangerous notions of binary opposition where one set would inevitably be honoured at the expense of the other. The back-jacket exclaims:

> This anthology greatly enlarges the contemporary scope of

> its predecessor. . . . It mirrors a remarkable decade in New Zealand writing. It also enlarges our understanding of what we mean by "contemporary."

In the excited claims for Evans's use of "contemporary," the jacket-writer implicitly reprimands McQueen for being narrowly concerned with fashion, discarding the past to consume the latest; and here I find the enthusiasm puzzling, for it seems to come from one of three causes.

First, it might represent a pre-emptive move to forestall criticism about including hundred-year-old texts in an anthology of contemporary literature by making such inclusion a virtue and a selling point.

Second, Evans's use of "contemporary" honestly strikes the jacket-writer as startling and revolutionary. This itself is startling, because it suggests that the past has been thoroughly dumped--no-one familiar with European-derived culture would find the notion of tradition as renewal either alien or novel. The jacket-writer's claim for the term suggests a de-cultured insensitivity, certainly to English language poetry (and to much of the English language poetry within the anthology itself) but also to the Maori poetry, which becomes the latest commodity in the cultural supermarket.

The English language poetry is often intensely alert to predecessors, whether to the demotic broadsheets Poole recovers, the landscape and "yarn" tradition which Newton and Dickson re-work, or the inheritance of an earlier generation of New Zealand poets writing in English. Dinah Hawken for instance re-writes the sonnet form, now so powerfully associated with Baxter and his religio-mythic vision. Leigh Davis too revises Baxter in poems from *Willy's Gazette* but for quite different ends from Hawken's quiet humanism. Davis's smart coterie work deconstructs the letter to offer in-joke allustions.

The blurb's implicit claim that "contemporary" and "tradition" are at odds serves to validate the Maori over the English language poets. Whether it does so deliberately or not, this is at once mischievous, misconceived and an accurate pointer to the kind of value which McQueen's Introduction seems to share and endorse.

About fifteen years ago, various critics and poets challenged

New Zealand writers to adopt the "open form" of poets from the United States.[5] The "open form" apologists claimed that they were not seeking to legislate for poetry, but that is what they effectually did. As in any effective advertising campaign, they aligned the product with irresistible qualities: vitality, daring, sexiness. The exciteness of being avant garde was stimulated through conjuring up as the "establishment" a figure who characteristically if curiously was both an effete old dodderer and an aggressive reactionary. If poets didn't write "open form" they might as well be buried, and would soon want to be.

The results are here. "I am reading *Rivers and Mountains*/ by John Ashbery" writes Rob Allan, and he is not alone. The spirits of Charles Olson, Robert Creeley and John Ashbery shadow each other through the new Penguin. Arguably fifteen years ago North American post-modernism liberated writers from a tyrannical poetic, now, however, the sameness of voice in some of the poetry suggests that a sensibility has become so entrenched as to represent a new hegemony.

Bill Manhire, discussing the influence of American poetry,[6] proposes that it is not influence which matters but the poem made from it. Yes, and the liveliness of some of the poetry in the Penguin anthology can perhaps be traced to North American poetry, which clearly many New Zealand poets find congenial. Nevertheless influence can disable. It does so when one kind displaces other forms from a writing community, when it distorts the representation of what, to use McQueen's words, "is happening in New Zealand verse," and when it cuts writers off from previous New Zealand poets writing in English. This latter becomes a possibility when "tradition" is understood as a chain which shackles the contemporary writer to the Greats of Europe with their matchless achievement. So Manhire reports that New Zealand writers had to free themselves from the dead weight of that European line if they were ever to produce fresh and local work, and American poetry helped achieve this breakthrough to plurality. (96)

As "tradition" is discounted, the value becomes "the new"-- which in New Zealand in the eighties came to mean post-Baxter. A theme that runs almost obsessively through Harry Rickett's collection of interviews with twelve New Zealand poets is the need to distance if not dismiss Baxter's poetry.[7] The reaction is inevitable given such a strong talent (whose work with its powerful local impress clearly is not weighed down but buoyed up by tradition). "Post" becomes not just a chronological marker but a cut-off point. If the concepts of "artist" or "inspiration" become discredited as part of an "elitist" discourse then what could dead poets say to us that we cannot say better ourselves? Progress has rendered the past irrelevant.

It is often claimed that post-modernist "open form" is an "ideologically aware" and "liberating" poetic. Perhaps it is. But it just as happily serves an economy of fashion and fast turnover. Despite claims that the anthology empowers marginalized groups and represents a public voice, (17) social comment is muted. The equable notation of sense-impressions, the liberal self-effacement, genial cataloguing, and clever de-construction, all deflect scrutiny, let alone the kind of scorching satire or Jeremiad found in some earlier New Zealand poems. I am not claiming that the presence of politics makes for good poetry, but suggesting that its absence indicates limits to an all too-dominant mode. The prevalent sensibility is at least as keen to efface clarity and simplicity as it is to avoid political comment.

I suggested a third possible cause behind the dust-jacket's remarks on "contemporary." Socratic naivety. And when you think about it why else are the remarks there, but to provoke us into seeing how "tradition" can work and has worked in conjunction with "contemporary"? We then find how poets like Dinah Hawkens and Leigh Davis, John Dickson, John Newton and Fiona Farrell Poole in their different ways re-writing the past, make it new. So the blurb offers its cunning and timely reminder that now English language poets, like their Maori colleagues, have an enabling New Zealand tradition. And the proof is their poetry which is post- not but also and-Baxter.

NOTES

1. See Peter Alcock, "Rites of Passage: New Zealand Poetry in Transition 1985-1987," *Journal of New Zealand Literature*, 5 (1987), pp. 29-44.
2. Harvey McQueen, and Ian Wedde, ed., *The Penguin Book of*

New Zealand Verse (Auckland: Penguin, 1985). Miriama Evans, Harvey McQueen, and Ian Wedde, ed., *The Penguin Book of Contemporary New Zealand Poetry. Nga Kupu Tituohu o Aotearoa* (Auckland: Penguin, 1989).

3. Murray Edmond, and Mary Paul, ed., *The New Poets of the 80's: Initiatives in New Zealand Poetry* (Wellington: Allen and Unwin/Port Nicholson Press, 1987). Louis Johnson, ed., *Antipodes New Writing* (Plimmerton: Antipodes Press, 1987). Mark Williams, ed., *The Caxton Press Anthology: New Zealand Poetry 1972-1986* (Christchurch: The Caxton Press, 1987). Lydia Wevers, ed, *Yellow Pencils: Contemporary Poetry by New Zealand Women* (Auckland: OUP, 1988).
4. *All Cretans Are Liars* (Auckland: AUP, 1987), *The Male As Evader* (Auckland: AUP, 1988). French has subsequently had a third book published, *Cabin Fever.*
5. See Arthur Baysting, ed., *The Young New Zealand Poets* (Auckland: Heinemann, 1973); C.K. Stead, "From Wystan to Carlos: Modern and Modernism in Recent New Zealand Poetry" (collected in his *In The Glass Case* (Auckland: OUP, AUP, 1981); Alistair Paterson, ed., *15 Contemporary New Zealand Poets* (Dunedin: Pilgrims South Press, 1980) and *The New Poetry* (Dunedin: Pilgrims South Press, 1981).
6. "Breaking the Line," in *The American Connection: Essays from The Stout Centre Conference,* ed. Malcolm McKinon (Wellington: Allen and Unwin/Port Nicholson Press, 1988).
7. *Talking About Ourselves: Twelve New Zealand Poets in Conversation with Harry Ricketts* (Wellington: Mallinson Rendall, 1986).

New Zealand Poetry from "Then" till "Now": "Wordsworth's Last Stand!"

ALAN RIACH

"Landscape Poetry" might be defined as the "unmediated associative contemplation of natural objects and perspectives through a heightened personal perception" and Wordsworth is its most familiar champion. Here he is, out on "An Evening Walk":

> How pleasant, as the yellowing sun declines,
> And with long rays and shades the landscape shines;
> To mark the birches' stems all golden light,
> That lit the dark slant woods with silvery white!
> The willows weeping trees, that twinkling hoar,
> Glanced oft upturned along the breezy shore,
> Low bending o'er the coloured water, fold
> Their moveless boughs and leaves like threads of gold;
> The skiffs with naked masts at anchor laid,
> Before the boat-house peeping thro' the shade;
> Th' unwearied glance of woodman's echoed stroke;
> And curling from the trees the cottage smoke.

By contrast, the tendency towards a poetry which I shall call "metonymic" is opposed to landscape poetry: it is a tendency away from the Romantic ideal of the clear apprehension of nature by the individual. It is, rather, a process of enmeshing the individual in the world of language, which provides us with the means to construct the economic, political and--perhaps most crucially for New Zealand--geographical structures, which produce significance. I say "significance," rather than "identity" because I find "identity" an over-used and underexplained term (both in Scotland and in New Zealand). In any case, it is not really applicable here. Identity is essentially a function of position, and position is, inevitably, a function of power. In the New Zealand context, the ramifications of that pattern of meanings might be taken to apply internally, to powerbased economic, political and racial structures. Internationally, they might apply to New Zealand's exemplary stance as an anti- as well as non-nuclear country, just as much as they apply to its lack of political pomp and swagger on the international stage. (One thinks of the international as opposed to the internal significance of ANZUS, and New Zealand's secession from United States foreign policy.)

What I'd like to do here is give a very brief overview--necessarily crude, necessarily prejudiced and necessarily incomplete--of New Zealand poetry from the mid-nineteenth century to now. I will concentrate mainly on Pakeha New Zealand poetry, but my argument applies in another way to Maori poetry written in English. It is, chronologically, a poetry which is understood as in some ways marginal to or dependent upon the "mainstream" tradition of English Verse--and I can make this clear by asking you to imagine how New Zealand poetry has been produced in relation to the two great Eurocentric cultural movements: Modernism and Romanticism. These two movements have shaped New Zealand poetry at crucial stages in a way that denies efforts to establish a purely autonomous nationalist line of "New Zealand" poetry. But at the same time both movements have been adapted to New Zealand imperatives, assimilated to essentially nationalist purposes. One might compare the relation of Scottish Literature to Romanticism and Modernism. Scottish writing contributed the most seminal *and* the most subversive influences upon the Romantic Movement, and there is an equally distinctive relation of Scottish writing to Modernism.)

I'd like to begin by looking at two early New Zealand poems, Edward Tregear's "Te Whetu Plains" and John Barr's "There's Nae Place Like Otago Yet." Tregear, 1846-1931, is the first poet in Vincent O'Sullivan's Oxford University Press *Anthology of Twentieth Century New Zealand Verse*, and "Te Whetu Plains" is pretty typical of a kind of landscape poetry which seeks to apprehend the land--New Zealand--and attempts to do so by adapting a Romantic or neo-Romantic posture. This fails, because nothing in the land responds to it.

All still, all silent, 'tis a songless land,
  That hears no music of the nightingale,
No sound of waters falling lone and grand
  Through sighing forests to the lower vale,
  No whisper in the grass, so wan, and grey, and pale.

When Earth was tottering in its infancy,
  This rock, a drop of molten stone, was hurled
And tost on waves of flames like those we see
  (Distinctly though afar) evolved and whirled
  A photosphere of fire around the Solar World.

Swift from the central deeps the lightning flew
  Piercing the heart of Darkness like a spear,
Hot blasts of steam and vapour thunder'd through
  The lurid blackness of the atmosphere.
  A million years have passed, and left strange quiet here.

Of course, the land Tregear found himself in could not possibly have been silent. Te Whetu Plains would have been full of birdsong. The poem is a completely artificial construct in which a Wordsworthian gesture of appeal is combined with a Byronic, independent alienation from such an idealist gesture. The posturing of the language discloses this ambivalence more than anything else.

Contrast a poem from some decades earlier--John Barr's "There's Nae Place Like Otago Yet." Barr was born in Paisley in 1809 and emigrated to Otago in 1852, where he died in 1899. He came out as a settler, an engineer turned farmer, not as a visitor: he came to stay, and his verse is part of his attempt to begin the process of re-establishing social priorities. "The work of John Barr expresses adequately the situation of the transplanted Scotsman," wrote James K. Baxter. Barr was the "acknowledged laureate" of the Otago province. He made it (just) into Allen Curnow's introduction to the influential 1960 *Penguin Book of New Zealand Verse.* "Having done well for himself, he sang the blessings of colonial life, contrasted with the poverty and inequalities of the old lands," Curnow wrote. "He is not unreadable today: on the other hand, his rhymes do not reveal to me . . . any special reason why he should be read." I think that's no longer true. We can see past Baxter and Curnow now to a different kind of vernacular poetry and a vigorous, demotic language. Moreover, his poems are evidence of an historical period of some significance, for Pakeha New Zealand lacks any native pre-capitalist past and Barr's poems appeared during New Zealand's originary era.

There's Nae Place Like Otago Yet

There's nae place like Otago yet
There's nae wee beggar weans,
Or auld men shivering at our doors
  To beg for scraps or banes.
We never see puir working folk
  Wi' bauchles on their feet,
Like perfect icicles wi' cauld
  Gaun starving through the street.

We never hear o' breaking stanes
  A shilling by the yard,
Or puir folk roupit to the door
  To pay the needfu' laird.
Nae purse-proud, upstart, mushroom lord
  To scowl at honest toil,
Or break it down that he, the wretch,
  May feast on roast and boil.

My curse upon them, root and branch
  A tyrant I abhor;
May despotism's iron foot
  Ne'er mark Otago's shore.
May wealth and labour hand in hand
  Work out our glorious plan,
But never let it be allowed
  That money makes the man.

The first thing one notices of course is that Barr's language is not English: the poem is in Scots. The linguistic idiom of the poem marginalizes itself, so to speak. The poem is placed on the periphery both of Scottish literature (itself, until recently, marginalized by English literature) *and* New Zealand Literature (as is shown by those comments of Curnow and Baxter, quoted above). This can be understood as a direct result of the poem's language. Other mid- or late-nineteenth century New Zealand poets did, in fact, choose to write in Scots (including one Jessie Mackay born in the South Island, a passionate advocate of Scottish home rule *and* feminism). But they have been largely forgotten or dropped from sight. Yet they are important for at least three related reasons: they demonstrate the degree of linguistic heterogeneity which went into New Zealand's formation and thereby they highlight the extent to which a uniform (if distinctive and idiomatic) *English* rapidly superseded such heterogeneity. They also draw attention to the political significance of that process, confirming Hugh MacDiarmid's diagnosis that "linguistic imperialism" sums up every other form of imperialism. And finally, they show that New Zealand is *not* a "bi-cultural" country, as so many have insisted in 1990, one hundred and fifty years after the Treaty of Waitangi (when the Maori did something similar to what the Scots did in 1707): rather, New Zealand is a *multi*-cultural country.

Barr's poem might seem to be no more than amusing doggerel--and that's how it can sound, if you recite it in a voice like that of John Laurie or as if it were mock-MacGonigallese. But if we look more closely for a moment we can see that the first verse actually offers a moving description--not of what Barr found *there*, in Otago, but of what he left behind in Paisley, or in Glasgow, the second city of the Empire (and in 1990, the widely-proclaimed "Cultural Capital of Europe"--the implications are worth pondering).

All of the first stanza and most of the second work by a process of inversion. In Otago, Barr says, there are no begging children, old men dying of hypothermia, workers frozen with cold, people too poor to afford to be properly clothed or sensibly shod, no conditions of starvation, or almost literal slavery--in short, the extremes of the mid-Victorian class system do not pertain. (It comes as no surprise that around the same time as I was turning this poem up in New Zealand, the Scottish poet Tom Leonard was rediscovering it in a library in Paisley, and it has since appeared in a valuable anthology edited by Leonard, entitled *Radical Renfrew*, as well as in the New Zealand literary journal *Landfall*, number 170.

The third stanza picks up on sentiments very familiar from Robert Burns and the neo-Burnsian tradition, and collapses into rhetorical gestures derived from "A man's a man for a' that": "The rank is but the guinea stamp, The man's the gowd for a' that!" But this democratic posturing is interesting in another way. Avoid the extremes of despotism and oppression, allow "wealth" and "labour" or work "hand in hand" and it will be possible to work out "our glorious plan." In other words, we must not abandon the class structure, but rather see that it works within sensible limits. The glorious plan might be the Protestant Work Ethic or a Puritan zeal for devotion to duty and enterprise, but it also suggests *literally* the "plan" of the city of Dunedin, which was built in Otago and based on a Scottish model. It was meant to be a palimpsest. The first settlers in Otago were a group of Scottish churchmen led by the Reverend Dr. Thomas Burns, nephew of the poet (a fierce old despot singing the psalms and hoping to found the place on "education, industry and above all, religion"). Dunedin was originally to be called New Edinburgh and the first settlers's ships, carrying 344 passengers, arrived in Port Chalmers in 1848--the same year, of course, as the publication of Marx and Engels's *The Communist Manifesto*. There is a modern American poet called Edward Dorn, whose short poem "Success?" seems appropriate enough to quote here:

Success?

I never had to worry about success
Coming from where I come from
You were a success the minute you left town.

Edward Tregear and John Barr provide examples of New Zealand poetry *then*--not great poetry, perhaps, but genuinely revealing. The history of New Zealand poetry from then till now has much more impressive things to offer, but certainly in the earliest period of colonial settlement, New Zealand poetry had lots to say about the nature of the land and its *distance* from "home." (If SPACE is, as another American poet, Charles Olson, said, the "first fact" to people born in America, perhaps DISTANCE has a similar function in New Zealand). And a necessary aspect of that sense of distance is the understanding of how what was written in New Zealand was written at a particular remove from the great literary movements that had taken place in the northern hemisphere: Romanticism and Modernism. (The same applies in a rather different way with Australian poetry.)

Perhaps the classic expression of this dilemma is Allen Curnow's "House and Land" and here I would like merely to draw attention to how this theme is worked into the poem in a very deliberately *literary* and *poetic* way. The connection to which I wish to draw attention is the reference Curnow makes to that far travelled Edinburgh-born writer Robert Louis Stevenson.

House and Land

Wasn't this the site, asked the historian,
Of the original homestead?
Couldn't tell you, said the cowman;
I just live here, he said,
Working for old Miss Wilson
Since the old man's been dead.

Moping under the bluegums
The dog trailed his chain
From the privy as far as the fowlhouse
And back to the privy again,
Feeling the stagnant afternoon
Quicken with the smell of rain.

There sat old Miss Wilson,
With her pictures on the wall,
The baronet uncle, mother's side,
And one she called The Hall;
Taking tea from a silver pot
For fear the house might fall.

People in the *colonies*, she said,
Can't quite understand . . .
Why, from Waiau to the mountains
It was all father's land.

She's all of eighty said the cowman,
Down at the milking-shed.
I'm leaving here next winter.
Too bloody quiet, he said.

The spirit of exile, wrote the historian,
Is strong in the people still.
He reminds me rather, said Miss Wilson,
Of Harriet's youngest, Will.

The cowman, home from the shed, went drinking
With the rabbiter home from the hill.

The sensitive nor'west afternoon
Collapsed, and the rain came;
The dog crept into his barrel
Looking lost and lame.
But you can't attribute to either
Awareness of what great gloom
Stands in a land of settlers
With never a soul at home.

That cowman "home from the shed" and his drinking-companion, the rabbiter "home from the hill" are echoes, palimpsests, of the sailor and the hunter in Robert Louis Stevenson's internationally famous and genuinely popular arch-Victorian "Requiem," which Stevenson wrote for himself and which most literate people for a number of generations picked up in childhood, and try as they might, remained unable to entirely forget:

Under the wide and starry sky
Dig the grave and let me lie.
Glad did I live and gladly die.
  And I laid me down with a will.
This be the verse you grave for me:
"Here he lies where he longed to be;
Home is the sailor, home from the sea
And the hunter home from the hill."

Curnow's cowman and rabbiter are very much *not* going to lie down where they "longed to be": they're going to get drunk to forget how far they are from anywhere they might call "Home."

New Zealand's most internationally acclaimed writer, Katherine Mansfield, also carries the same theme through--in her bardic, large-gestured poem addressed to the Polish patriotic playwright Stanislaw Wyspianski--which begins

> From the other side of the world,
> From a little island cradled in the giant sea bosom,
> From a little land with no history,
> (Making its own history, slowly and clumsily
> Piecing together this and that, finding the pattern, solving the problem,
> Like a child with a box of bricks),
> I, a woman, with the taint of the pioneer in my blood,
> Full of a youthful strength that wars with itself and is lawless,
> I sing your praises, magnificent warrior; I proclaim your triumphant battle.

It is here, I think, that one might understand how New Zealand poetry turns from *then* to *now*. Mansfield takes us to the heart of the problem.

She is, after all, firstly *acclaimed* as a writer of major importance in the pantheon of international modernism--but she is also *claimed* by various different critical factions whose function is to define the literature they study against certain criteria. She is claimed, for example, by different *national* literatures--English literature, French literature, and of course New Zealand literature; she is claimed by feminists as a Woman Writer; she has been deconstructed and post-structuralized, and generally subjected to a range of critical procedures. She is, of course, not fully "contained" by any one of these methods of appraisal. She lived as a writer at exactly the time when estrangement and exile were becoming commonplace and normal conditions--and of course many of the great writers of modernism were exiles.

And since--shall we say--1945, these conditions have developed to such an extent that it is now *more* normal for poetry in New Zealand as elsewhere to dress for international travel than for the local bushwalks. The process I mentioned at the start of this paper--away from the ideal of direct apprehension of the immediate and local towards the valorization of the uncentred and marginal--seems far advanced. And if I have characterized New Zealand poetry *now* as being primarily "metonymic" I should just quickly explain what I mean by that term. It is simply a figure of speech by which we understand a word or a phrase to mean something it is related to, and stands for: we might say "the bottle" when we mean "a drink." What that depends upon, of course, is a *shared* understanding of how the language works. It is at the furthest remove from that famous example in Wordsworth's "The Thorn"--where Wordsworth describes a small pool of water in the wilderness and asserts his objectivity by claiming to have measured it exactly:

High on a mountain's highest ride,
Where oft the stormy winter gale
Cuts like a scythe, while through the clouds
It sweeps from vale to vale;
Not five yards from the mountain-path,
This thorn you on your left espy;
And to the left, three yards beyond,
You see a little muddy pound
Of water, never dry;
I've measured it from side to side:
'Tis three feet long, and two feet wide.

Yet contemporary New Zealand poetry, if it deals, generally, with language and systems that are now part of the literate person's vocabulary internationally, is still drawing on these familiar themes. An example of how persistent they are is Bill Manhire's very gentle and moving poem, "A Scottish Bride."

A Scottish Bride

Long division and underprivilege,
sweets in a paper twist; or later,
hiking in the hills, days

like the fizz of flowers in a vase
she carried to a neighbour's house,
a war bride with a photograph of home,

and her own house on a single pulse
of stone, lapped by the tidal starlight.
Whose days were those?

A lit hearth, the flames trod water,
and on the dresser a wedding-cake
ascended like a genealogy towards

the two small figures on the top,
standing beside a silver flower
which gave them back a blurred reflection.

Were those the circumstances
which would have to change? A daughter
rehearsed expressions in the mirror,

choosing the face she might prefer to hold,
another touched the perforations
of a stamp, a profile she was saving.

You cannot imagine, halfway
across the world, her father wrote,
the sorrow of the undersigned. Was that her mother

then, who made those numbers on a slate?
Were those her children, almost finished eating,
blowing upon their faces in the spoons?

A modest and gentle competence informs the project of Manhire's poetry and a fine sensibility of discrete, fragmented histories prevails in his poems. The four questions which punctuate "A Scottish Bride" are not asked insistently but quietly press senses of distance and difference further into your consciousness: "her own house on a single pulse/ of stone, lapped by the tidal starlight./ Whose days were those?" The question probes tenderly, without striving to find answers with which to bridge the gulfs the poem evokes.

A lit hearth, the flames trod water,
and on the dresser a wedding cake
ascended like a genealogy towards

the two small figures on the top . . .

"Genealogy" is a particularly well-chosen word. The distinction between a nostalgia for origins and the concerns of genealogy has been discussed by Michel Foucault. Foucault argued that the Nietzschean genealogist is concerned with the gaps, the lapses, the intensities, the agitations, in short the discontinuity (the distances) and not some thread that links history with an origin. In this the genealogist is indifferent to the quest for the "father" or the "origin." (One might contrast the much more urgent sense of "originality" in Curnow's poetry.) The genealogist always lives in uncertainty and any genealogy is an asymptote. (Manhire himself claims to be a Scots-Cornish amalgam.)

This uncertainty is deftly suggested in "A Scottish Bride." The father writing of "*the sorrow of the undersigned*" acknowledges the human grief these distances give rise to. The question immediately following restores the naiveté of an incomprehension on the part of the grown daughter, now a mother herself, the Scottish Bride of the title: "Was that her mother/then, who made those numbers on a slate?" (That carefully inflected word "then" affords the perception of an ambivalence in time and meaning, as it signifies "so long ago" as well as "therefore, after all.")

The sense of distance, the sense of isolation: clichés perhaps but cornerstones of New Zealand Poetry--and touched here with a sense of human frailty, and human resilience. If the questions are unanswered they are not unasked. Generations have arisen asking them.

I'll end with a couple of poems of my own. "The Blues" is a not entirely serious kind of love poem. It was written in Hamilton, in New Zealand; the river is the Waikato and there is a reference to the Silver Fern Rail Service, but aside from these local references, the poem has an obvious general application I didn't think I need to explain:

The Blues

The lights are on all over Hamilton.
The sky is dark, blue
as a stained glass window in an unfrequented church
say, by Chagall, with grand and glorious chinks
of pinks and purples,
glittering jewels on those glass fronted buildings
where the lifts are all descending
and the doors are
being closed.
  You're out there somewhere,
going to a concert in wide company or maybe
sitting somewhere weaving a carpet
like a giant tapestry, coloured grey,
pale brown, weaving the wool
back in at the edges of the frame, your
fingers deft as they turn the wool in tight and
gentle curves.
          Or somewhere else.
          What do I do
          except imagine you?
          The river I keep crossing
          keeps going north. The trains
          in the night cross it too.
          Their silver carriages are blue.

And "At Spirits Bay, the Empty Sea." This is a "landscape" poem--but in the extent to which it relies on referentiality it is at the furthest remove from Wordsworth's unmediated contemplation (which is not to say it's in any sense preferable). The objective measurements with which Wordsworth circumscribed his concerns in "The Thorn" are foreign to this poem: nor is it a rhapsodic description, in the manner of the poem with which I began this paper, "An Evening Walk." Rather, it asks for a particular kind of vision, one which possesses an understanding of how memory and "dimensionality" work in language, and which then can focus in particular ways, while running through the poem keeping up a pleasurable speed.

Spirits Bay is so named because of its proximity to the most northerly point of the North Island of New Zealand, Cape Reinga, from which the spirits of the Maori dead are said to depart, on their way to the ancestral home island of Hawai'iki. (I have been told that Invercargill serves a similar function for Pakeha New Zealanders.)

Now, this poem was published round about the same time in Scotland, in the annual anthology *New Writing Scotland*, and in New Zealand, in the quarterly *Landfall*. When the *New Writing Scotland* anthology was reviewed in the *Edinburgh Review*, the anonymous reviewer singled it out for special mention, commenting that one would have to be a New Zealander to understand it. I found this amusing enough to show to one of the editors of *Landfall*, Iain Sharp, who, noting that the poem had been published in New Zealand as well, suggested that he might write a letter to the *Edinburgh Review* pointing out that it was the opinion the poetry-reading public in New Zealand that to understand this poem one would have to be a Scot.

Be that as it may, the poem seems to be offering pleasures as well as difficulties and it has, I believe, pleased readers as much as it has puzzled them. One of the pleasures involved in surely piecing together the references and quotations, from Charles Olson, Herman Melville, Ralph Waldo Emerson: and one of the puzzles, perhaps, is how much or how little one's knowledge of the operations of such quotations add anything at all to the poem.

At Spirits Bay, the Empty Sea

"You cannot miss the ships that miss each other
ships that the wide earth parts"
  the sliding waters meet
them all, and all the ships come in.
   The Tasman nudges off the Cape
   the sallow stern of long Pacific slants.
   The Cape runs ragged down the land
   and susurrates into the oceans;
   Auratic, yet the sand is scald, is
   beaten gold, the rocks as black,
   the grasstopped hill

bright emerald, the lighthouse
lighthouse-white.

"Have I come these 20,000 miles
to be beaten by an empty wind?"
(The ruin or the blank in our own eye.
The axis of vision is not coincident
with the axis of things. Therefore the words (world)
lacks unity. Said Emerson. He sang:
Don't fence me in. The palisades
suround the lighthouse.
Even out there
where the 2 seas say hello
to each other they're shaking hands
with rippling knuckles, as
white as waves are
on cobalt.

Good as Gold

Those deaths of Mahler's cypress-lined
Adagios. What can you do with them
In New Zealand? Pohutukawas
Are too flash for death or *angst*,
They grow too fast for *abschied.*
Chekhov's another problem here.
There's no money and the orchard's
For the chop. The man in real estate
Has an answer no-one wants to hear:
'Music please,' he tells the Jews.
Back to Paris, she'll be right.
Come to think of it, maybe Chekhov's
Not a problem in New Zealand.

MARSHALL WALKER

Pioneers--Kirikau

Note: Kirikau is a small settlement about twenty miles down Wanganui river from Taumarunui. The large isolated area around it was offered for sale to soldiers returning from the First World War. Its name denoted "the place where a battle was fought by men stripped naked"--an irony which seems to have gone unnoticed.

Late 1989 we made a pilgrimage back to the place where some of the family had spent their summer holidays as children, helping on the "farms" wrested from the forests. These poems are a response to the journey. For me it was the first time I had been in that part of the country. For Bill it meant going back some sixty years.

All the people in the poems have now gone, but the land, in part, and scarred, remains.

Bert

He was the second son. At twenty-five
he'd lived more than a life. Three years
in Egypt, Paschendale and right through
to Verdun and Ypres. Wipers
the boys called it and many were.
His oldest brother also. The sun
in his mother's eye. She never shone
again. Her mouth hooked
hard as the kettle over the range
in the kitchen where she darkened her days.
For a while he bore corpses and the blown
up bits of friends on stretchers
across battlegrounds. Afterwards
he never sat still for a minute. Even the chair
was straightbacked and hard.
When morale was down he was one of the boys
in the band trading canonshot for timpani. Another

kind of thunder he later made his living
in the silent movies. When it was over
he baked five hundred pancakes with what small supplies
were left for the troops and drank one glass
of beer. All his life he'd learned
to be frugal. His one indulgence
a goose he walked on Sundays
in a suit and never ate. Mostly he wanted
to make up the lost years and drove a De Soto
at mind breaking speed. The point
to set your goal and get there fast. He made it
past ninety.

Reg

There are different versions
of what happened. In one story
they don't tell you how he had the bastard
rammed up in the race. Its horns caught
in the space between the 8 x 2's. Took an axe
and chopped them off. Better than mending
the rails and couldn't be bothered
to traipse all the way back
for tools. Besides they'd expect him home
for tea, pass the cakes round
for the ladies. He was very good
at dancing and wore small shining
patent-leather feet to wing the night
away. On Saturdays
he dressed in white for cricket
Sometimes he boiled
live eels in cauldrons. They screamed
but what the hell, he'd heard it all
before at Paschendale.
When his best dog took to worrying the sheep
he bashed its head in with a fence post.
Didn't want to go all the way
to the shed for a gun and no point

in having feelings. A man might die
that way. Sometimes at night
he thought the clouds frowned, the river
talked, but he knew it was only water
over the stones where the moon caught
the ripple of rapids laughing
round the bend. Next morning
he would blast the course and build a wall
to change the current
still the voices.

Tawata

Here maps fail and history confuses. Also
the manner it records. Mostly you listen to stories
told from under trees, the way a stone talks
in your hand. Sometimes you see how
the wind lies from a twisted branch. The willows
say the missionary felt homesick with his darkness
struggling up the river. Imagined himself back
"gently down the stream." Maybe he wanted light
relief in seasons, spring spectaculars in all that
grim foreboding, the messages he brought.
Also Tawa is sombre the books tell you
now there's not much left but stumps
that "sit upon the ground and tell sad stories
of the death of kings." Other legends
speak of beatings and a woman picking fruit.
Scars are visible, also in those early pictures.
What possessed them you wonder to spend
their days slashing their way to the sky.
When the light fell all they could see was black
and columns of smoke rising. For a moment
the men might have thought they were back
at Paschendale but they were not given
to fancy, kept their heads down and went on
fighting. Sometimes they scratched an entry in a diary,
took a photo. Mostly the smiling is just round the corner

and you can't imagine why they dressed
for picnics on the charred persistent trunks rising
like Goya *Disasters* from the torn ground.
Zadkine is there turning up his question marks
towards the beggared sky, but Edith smiles
"sitting on a stump," the height of a man
in her best clothes. Even now the captions in their albums
lie their way from one book to another:
"The raw slips in the hills behind
were caused by rain."

Bill
(Pehimahaka)

This is where the road ends and your journey
begins again in the going back. You tell us stories
and the fires sweep through this first burn.
It is summer and the heat is unbearable. We try
to keep to whatever shade has grown again
through the years you were in other landscapes,
watch the smoke curling into the hearts of family
and hardening the small arteries of love. We see
eyes narrow. Shoulders sharp chiselled
against the felled spaces. At night
a million tears fall from the fleeing sky.
We ask questions and you answer. The map
on your face does not give
many directions. You keep it close
as if pointing the past is painful and you are afraid
an icy wind will suddenly bluster across these bare summer
records of loss. A kereru knells
and our eyes follow a fence-line you helped tighten.
You were eight, maybe younger. You carried the hammers.
Even the horse couldn't make it
and stumbled over torn ground stretching up forever.
You thought the peak reached into heaven. It took days
lugging everything up. The wire clawed and ripped.
The posts heavier than crosses. You learned

your first lessons here and as you tell the story
we watch the hammer somersaulting all the way
down to where we are at the bottom of the gulley
and a small boy falling to fetch it and starting
the long climb back. Sheep are white flecks
against that barren hill where your fence struggles
now to keep upright. It has weathered
sixty years. I look at your hands. Fine lines net
together the fragile web of past, threading in and out
through lives watching from shadows.
At night we cook the pehu found growing wild
on the river flat. Our small circle of stones a ritual
fire. The hills crouch darkly. They too are
remembering stories where the sun overturned
and blazed through nights shrill with panic and birds
fleeing from the vanished sky.
They eye the glowing tongues suspiciously, anxious
to see the Upoko-roa children won't suddenly leap out
and break into that devastating language echoing
still from their ochre slurring scars.

Note: Me oioi ki te ringa ka puta te tama a Upoko-roa. When the hand is moved backwards and forwards the child of Upoko-roa appears--the reference is to the action of rubbing a firestick. Upoko-roa, or Long-Head is the personification of comets.

Endings

Much later they built a proper house
up from the river. Everyone came from town
to help. It took the whole summer.
Each day the kids let the current rush
them down the rock-bend, climb up the bank and run
back through the paddock, sliding in under
the willow that held out its hands full of gifts for Tutagata-
kina sleeping with one open eye under Taniwha Rock.
You knew it was there from the eddies, all that swirling
water, like on washday in the copper, trying to pull you under.

That's how Sam died Arthur reckoned. Must have
caught pneumonia after a day's hot work. He was only thirty
and a big man at that. Should have known
How the water was always cold and disapproving,
how you had to be on the look-out for snags
and the ice-sharp teeth that sank right through your bones
and made you gnaw with pain all over. At night too
it spooked there with stories and sometimes you heard
the trees giggling together but all you saw was stars.
Sometimes they found an ancient tool of war
and hung it on the mantle with the gun. They shot
down rapids in a dug-out log yelling
to dispel their fright. On Christmas the men got in
a dozen beer and twice the lemonade for shandies.
They took the empties all the way back a hundred
and thirteen miles down river. A tiny ritual
signalling the end of summer. Those who stayed
went back to six days slog a week.
On Sundays they tidied up the flower garden.
Arthur put an orchard in. Something
out there had made him harsh, and nearly all his
children left. He didn't have the temperament
but loved his fruit trees. It was something
he was good at. The ash from the burns made the onions
grow. He also dug potatoes.
Apples, plums and pears. Apricots perhaps
(the stories differ and nobody much wrote down
the facts). Walnuts from a fellow further down
who lost his acres to the *Loan & Mercantile*, or maybe
from his brother back in town
who carted kernels every time he came up river.
When the old man left and moved to town
his son ran chainsaw through the trees and ripped
the orchard out. Couldn't bear the sight
of his father. Sheep graze there still but down the road
wild apples bloom.

Kirikau

No trees obstruct the view. All has been
cleared away to give the hawk full range
to skim across the scraped clean hills. They
needed wood for timber. The rest they burned.
Next spring they made small clouds
with scattering seeds of grass. We stop
at a bend in the road to remember
a Maire felled and taken out by sledge
and horse. In the photographs
nobody tells you how long it took, how everything
ached, how the earth howled, feeling its scalp ripped
open by the tearing roots. So few of them
were taken unawares. Most are formal. Smiling
men spread-legged on falling kings, riding
to muster through a slaughter of charred remains
shrounded always in smoke. Their hats obscure
their faces, cast shadows across eyes that might
have told. Certainly they were not sentimental.
Trees were sheds and houses, fence and palings
round a grave to keep out pigs. Also
they were suspicious of strangers and wanted to see
them coming. The curtain always slightly pushed
aside. The door pulled to, in case. An axe
ready at the back, a shotgun slung above
the mantle. A lean-to for gumboots. That's where
they washed the dishes, carting the water from up river
when the tanks ran dry. There was never enough
to go round. They washed their feet in puddles.
The copper took priority. It ruled the house. Women
were seen bowing over its boiling ("bubble, bubble
toil and trouble.") They touched its tarnished sheen
with polish and burned eternal fires. Also the range
was stoked all day. It was a bit like living
in hell.

RIEMKE ENSING

Voyage Out: Liverpool to Port Chalmers, N.Z., 1863
An Early Diarist (of The Voyage Out)

1

Peasoup and pork today and a little girl's dying.
Corpse on a board put over at sunrise,
covered with flag and tipped into the sea.
We came to the poop to sing hymns. On Christmas
we saw islands, more peasoup and pork
and another one's sewn in his canvas, dropped
into the depths--a married man too, seven children
left, the youngest at breast. Thunder and lightning.
And boat covered with clothes, sea air is sweet.
All's happy today and a good many drunk.
New Year we're crossing the line, and dancing tonight.
There's a young woman gone wrong in her mind
but no place to put her. Among us she shrieks.
Becalmed, then the trade winds, heat hard to stand.
Six Sabbaths at sea, and the silly girl's dead.
A death's little thought of. In ten minutes
it's the same on deck or below, and a boy about three.
Death is so dull, very many on board. I sit
in my muslin, little more in the heat and sea breeze.
All on board very sick. I got wet and my thumb hurt.

2

Dreadful heat but fine concert, about six play the flute,
three bagpipes, one fiddle. Bad night, ship becalmed,
then stormy again. Tenth Sabbath at sea, many a long look
for the Cape--men climbed up masts. A shark caught this morning
then two little wee ones. A good many folk sick--not a fair wind.
Great sea birds sail round us--two young men are ill.
Sea dashing right over us some falling down, getting wet.
Passed a large ship with sails up, heading for Sydney.
John Dickie--six months--is put overboard. Fine Breeze
and a seabird was captured. The women are fine, very friendly.
Sea was rolling like mountains, high at times as the sails

and we rocked to and fro very badly. Now and then you could
ride smooth as a boat in a pond, very safely. Singing was done
before bed. In the daytime all bring their beds on the deck,
get them sweetened with air. Pumps keep the decks clear
but we heave and pitch tremendously. I will not close my eyes.
When I dream it is ships and they sink in the sand
and I claw towards the trees on the shore and cannot reach one.
When I wake there are whimpers, and that mother calms babes.
I suspect they miss father, and she misses him too.

3

Plenty of meat but ship rolling all night, makes tins
toss all about. Captain comes in now and then for a joke.
We have a good light when we're sick, whale oil in a pot.
When on deck I am always blown over. I hope will be better.
Storm tumbling and I wish it was calmed. I got flipped
out of bed. Water dashes on bunks--such a crying some thought
we were sunk. But they bored holes to take it away.
Captain is kindly, came down to see us our time in distress.
Then it was past and said we need not fear as he looks
night and day after us and we are not near great rocks.
Sang a song and made prayers but Oh it was a strain
ever since we sailed it has been that. Fine morning but calm.
No want but nothing well cooked--baked loaves
and some dumplings. Plenty of raisins, so no want here yet.
Must put up with our troubles, all fainting in bed.
Smallpox may break out, but I hope it will not.
I am sitting on poop and all looks happy today.
But oh dear, we are poor of land, nothing but sea,
nothing but sky. Still all is pleasant. Met two ships
that we cheered. Captain performed on the flying trapeze.

4

Put up our three flags, sea washing on decks then like
a Spring day. Sun so warm and dinner is good--met a ship
in full sail, the preacher not well. I think of them that I
left back in Glasgow, may the Lord be with them as well.

What I'd give to hear Sherwood, yet that cannot be.
I know it cannot--may the Good Lord be with him.
Not a fair wind, that makes it worse, raining a bit.
Peasoup and pork and another man's ill. He came
for his health, died about five. Solemn sight
he's put over at dawn, corpse laid on a board
put over to sea, a lesson to mark--we may soon meet God.
Came back to the poop to sing hymns. Preacher sang best.
Ship rolls back and forth, from one side to the other.
Water's turned red and cold rain's not so cheering,
a scone with our tea. Wave splashed me all wet.
Men's bonnets blew off and they swam on the deck.
We got oatmeal and sugar and pork and peasoup,
nice pie as cook's gift, crumbly brown scones so we had
a good tea. Sea coming in hatch, we hold on for dear life.
Man fell on port deck, surgeon sewed up his lip.

5

Never storm worse than this. Sailors got
our fresh water, we keep to our beds. Rice soup
for our dinner, no calm on the sea.
A man got sore hurt--some ropes fell and smashed him.
Today killed a pig, all young women got some.
Two more to kill yet, they belong to the First Class.
Sailors pulling down sails, raining and dull-like--
still very cold. Another girl dead, now that mother has six,
first her husband, now child, put over at seven,
died at one in the morning. And another today, young man
age eighteen--had no friends. God make us ready.
All at once a hail shower, great squall of wind
and Captain no coat nor a bonnet cried "All hands on deck!"
And water was level with boat--great reason to fear,
then cleared up and the moon shone all through the night.
We are close every minute to calm and to death. Cannot sleep
when it's stormy. Still a fair wind, heaving a great deal.
Fifteenth Sabbath on board, long time at sea. Potatoes again.
More raisins they say our last week, will make us look good.
We're busy at hats, sorting our bonnets and looking for land.

6

Soda scones and some ham, oatmeal sausage and tea, enjoyed
very well. Large fish jump:d about. Captain's dog
went mad, shut him up in his cabin, jumped out
and was drowned. Such a wave coming over I nearly was washed
over, then calm. All looking for land. Saw a ship far away.
Then saw Snare Island--nothing but rocks. Cry of land,
so I went up to poop and saw hills. Flour and meal with our tea,
splendid sight of the hills. Been sailing all day
in sight of the land. Young woman died, got consumption
on board. Hills all covered with trees. Matron's daughter
put over and us near our landing. And we anchored at ten,
a place called Port Chalmers, saw houses close to the sea,
pretty place. Steamer came close, will take us the rest
of the way to Dunedin And when we arrived such a lot
came to see us. But not a face that I knew. Nice place indeed!
Immigration man said all us females are good class--equal
number of town servants, country, and fine breeding stock
who will soon be engaged. He has no doubt, so he said, signed
a paper and sealed it. Said he was humble, a servant himself.
But I think he is not. Thanks to God we are safe, minus eighteen.
But I never did think it would be like it is, what it is now.

Teaching the Snow

Five minutes before class
I dog-ear the page of each poet
who's been in a madhouse, and I sight
like a glacier a vision of those blank pages
spread like snow--silence and snow
rather than books that might have been born,
poems written by men ordered to give their minds rest
or women told not even to think, much less write--
to keep their journals blank, abandon their diaries
and travel nowhere that might stir the primal monsters
that lurk in the brain. I imagine great sunny slopes--
white snow of oblivion they might have left us

instead of their pages so monstrous, so tortured.
Suddenly an immense power inflames me.
I stalk into the room with the Word
blinding us, the class taught in silence.
And for once the great lesson takes hold.

The Giant Bird that Could Not Fly Away from His Destiny
After Allen Curnow

Gazing at the skeleton of the giant moa
it was not down to the great egg I looked,
repaired somehow after its millions
of years in fragments, nor at the two claws
like pitchforks that had walked so much
primeval mud, but up, up, up to the bones
of the neck aspiring as if at last I would get
to myself, ourselves--where we are now,
were then, looking about from our height--
we the point all creatures of the sea swam
toward. Slugs and lungfish aspired to be us. Did not
wings of birds eagerly beat to make us angelic
with our bright eyes still on rickety, frail
legs propped, fragile and breakable
in this museum of the world, watchful for the next
cloud that will break us, ash that will shroud us.
But this time without the great bird for companion.

Aluminium

At Aramoana across the bay from the albatross nest
all the rooftops were ablaze with signs
to save the shores and air--not let them build
that much-touted smelter that would foul the air unduly.
Setting their aluminium cans down on tables
at the Robbie Burns Pub, New Zealand's best poets shouted
out protest. The peninsula had to be saved--
and they managed it. The devils withdrew for the nonce.

But they'll be back, some say, when we're closer
to living like rats, when there's more rubble, when we can't
afford to care so much. And they'll bring to this nuclear-
free land their ships that leak hell. In any case,
the shores are safe for the moment--the prospect of gulls
stumbling drunk with disease from aluminium deferred
for a while, along with fears the albatross might forget
(if he ingested the dust of that stuff) how to perform
the ecstatic courtship display. Even people are safe, though a
successful protest could not have been built
upon them. The birds are more clearly treasures,
and the songs sung in their praise far more persuasive.

A Day with Baxter: His Home in New Zealand
"No desire is ever answered except by death."

James K. Baxter

Quite sober on Sunday we stood on the cliff
where Baxter said he considered suicide

and I had no reason to doubt him. Far below,
green bullkelp uncurled immense hydra-like

arms, pale in the sun. White surf beyond
embroidered the blue Pacific. Farther out,

a lone ship etched the horizon and I travelled
on to America where our little black dog

might be dreaming of sheep. He never
in his life has seen one, yet in green parks

he runs in circles--chasing sheep of the air,
avatars of his deep ancestral memory-skills

intact in his genes. We spoke of how happy
he would be in New Zealand with authentic

lambs to charm him and how in a previous life
he may have known this island where we walked

Baxter's hills--so much like the South Downs
of your Sussex, for all this nation is England

imagined, rebuilt to survive should catastrophe
strike, some terrible Blitz suffered anew.

We ascend the dirt road the poet strolled
drunk in moonlight, or sobering up about noon.

I hear dry broom pods pop, flinging seed
to the air, for those blooms yellow and bold

as melting butter are gone for this year.
Grief is sharp. We know we are leaving,

will not see this gold when it blooms. We spot
in the valley work of an Irishman who shovelled

peat out till long duck-lanes spelled a message--
slash of wild calligraphic wit to be read

from the sky. He wrote for the ducks, geese,
albatross. Baxter had no hammerhead shovel,

no peatbog, yet filled with ink frenzied books
as truth kept edging out just beyond him, bird

of mind's air. He knew that one gull's wing
swooping achieved more than man could.

Write on water, indeed! All of us, on air!
And soon gone, while encoded on feathers, fossils

deep in stone, the poem's finished, perfected.
No wonder Baxter despaired, as we must

who seek our Jerusalem here. Now and then
my albatross wings unfurl and I swoop off

the cliff. On that ridge over Brighton,
Baxter's village, we stood and inhaled a few

of his lines, saw his sea calm and serene
in the distance, tortured up close, its marriage

with rocks, bullkelp lashed by wave breaking.
Not even Baxter made sense of all this.

On the way down we looked toward his house,
the room where he paced, its glass opalescent,

sun-struck, backlit warped windows aglow, rainbows
where for a moment I saw Baxter, still at work.

Then I thought of him bearded, serene
in his coffin while hippy friends of that year

sat around him--sipping a last tea with their master.

At the Home of James K. Baxter, New Zealand Poet

It's a bay that would be thought lonely
only by those who make no allowance
for the company of gulls, the tussock butterfly,
the great charm of sea, the occasional drifters
called swagmen--hoboes strolling over the brow
of a hill, much like the Downs of England
though more sheep browse here, far more--
often on their knees to graze. The poet too
nibbles horizon, gulps in blue sky,
and comes at last to understand
how the sea never makes a mistake,
those white knuckles drumming.

Toward the Smile
for Brian Turner

"Watching the blessed ones move far off,
and the smile on God's face."

Yeats, quoted by James K. Baxter

As Baxter is not among us
we must find Baxter
in one another. "Silence
is the only voice,"
he wrote at Aramoana
where I found a gull
dead on the pier, at peace,
a little feathered cradle
of gentleness. On the hill above
at another of those sessions
in the green and blue that so outdo
stained glass and the Oamaru stone
of cathedrals, I saw a white sheep--
his wool blown in wind, his leg
bone torn away, his skull
black as if by fire. My son--
whose face was black
before I could reach him--
is a white sheep on a hill now.
Peace is a long time coming
and we need all the silence
we can get, the forgiving communion
of friendship. Let Baxter
be with us as we walk this hill,
along with those others we write for--
your blessed ones and mine--
letting them glow through us
with that silence no word
can quite touch though we give
our lives daily seeking it,
passing the emptiness.

Friend, walk beside me,
Let our silence drift over the dead.
Let us never withdraw
surf of our love from their shores.

The Asylum at Seacliff

for Janet Frame

Not the first entombed there, with view
of sea through the bars, sea that would mirror
all moods, silver shining upon it
or world crumpled, discarded like trash,
windblown. Those who pried her hands loose,
who strapped her on table, who held pad
in her teeth, told her not to look
on such wreckage, what floats to shore
from worlds too far to care for. She saw
how they mocked mind, hers that they said
they cared for, the one that came up
with thoughts they labelled "bizarre,"
not worth the thinking. As for them, they
would not seek God in a chimney,
hear lost voice in a gull wheeling close.

Let there be life without vast green
was their wisdom, they who took crayons
from left hand, placed them in right.
Let there be boredom--they all but said so.
Let there be sane joy of tea,
ecstasy of cake and grey morning.
Let her speak in that soft voice bland
as custard, a blankness achieved.
Let the brother be lost in war, sister
be left face down in the pool. But let weeping
be done with. And the success
was that she gave it all up--the poem
and nine-tenths of the hurt, kept silver spoons
shined and gleaming, cut the cake thin.

A slice lay on her hand for a moment,
then fell on the plate like a brick wall
intact as she turned her taut smile
to the tourist. What was left
of the passionate pilgrim was the deep pool
shé drew from. She offered a refill,
even a smile, sang out thanks for the tip.

DAVID RAY

Bali Rice & Sky

Rice

Lean your ear
down close-
its breath's

as rhythmic as
sloshy snortings
of water buffalo

or seedlings
swishing
a farmer's muddy legs.

Sky

The sky is a poem.
The stars of the plough
hold up the sky.

If every word
were a grain of rice
poets could feed Asia.

Moon Mad

to Li Pai
who tried to hold the moon

You, the night-dancer
try to clutch her.
Her saffron spills
the powder clings
to lily stems.
The fish are golden.
She spins in your hands.

You swallow your mind.

The pond is water-black.

Sky Crosses, Singapore

I have this rectangle of sky to look into
off my balcony ten floors up.
Two pointers go directly to the Southern Cross
(but can I be sure it isn't false cross
that I'm not tipped over, half-way round
the world from home and seeing askew?)

Well, maybe instead, that's it, off to the left
and those original transversals are the pointers?
No, not bright enough and not enough stars
or dark to see with. Anyway, there's
too much interference from down here
runway lights, heights of building lights

Showing you the way to go, you can only see
just in front of you, something's not
quite opened up enough about it all
you can't get any sort of fix through it.
At home, you look straight up and see it
know immediately where you are,

breathe the air, pick up the idiom.
Irina Ratushinskaya says limited human rights
are as impossible as limited breath.
You're free or not, you breathe or don't.
She composed her poems on soap bars,
memorised the lines then washed them off.

They smiled, the women, when led
to solitary, knowing the others,
though weakened by the times before,
would fast for them, knowing fredom

is to know where you stand
in a whole sky, no rectangles.

Appeasement

for Jayanta Mahapatra

To read you is to walk India.
Cows wander in and out of your poems
cripples and beggars lurch along
to sleep, die and be re-born
between steps, between words.

You say you're too much a coward
can't give up enough of self
to do more, must first write
to appease. Lacking faith, you
record the illiterate faithful

whose trance-swallowed tongues
speak only to Lord Shiva.
Their shuffing feet kick up
your muttered mantras
to dance, dustmotes in light.

Self Portrait

I remind myself of Emily Dickinson
locked in the attic of my thoughts
with the casement window flung out open
onto the night air & he who gives me breath

or I'm Heathcliff's girl downed in heather
& the moors pound under me like the purple
galloping surf on a West Coast beach
& romance catches me in the throat again

and I can't unsay it, though I want

the words to tell that this silent well
in me is years strong and filtered
by doubt, gainsaying and turning away.

But who can turn from the truth? It
faces you with the etchings, gouaches
and monoprints in the gallery of your life.
He's the big one down on the farthest wall.

You Hoped It Is Love In Your House

for Anna in Basel

Not only love, love distilled
springs in the acacia, where the mind's winter birds
wake to parties in summer gardens;
goldfish breed in the daisies
& a rabbit swims through uncut grasses.

The sun's steep over the roof way down under
from where the moon's come
so quickly up a hemisphere.
She moves bellyful through the wheatfields.
Did anyone ever name her quite rightly?
She's a swan.

Schubert swells in every room
where each can return to self.
A bubbling in the ventricles
blood of the lamb, some call it
that wine at meeting, at parting.
At home, *arohanui*, great love

we now say, for what the birds tune to
remind us we and they are made of, we turn to.

Suttee

All this love flaming from me,
as if angel voices lit me,
I am dying for,
white song, white pyre,
white piercing the shrieked air.

In my widow's burning robes,
I go, to breathe
only as the sky,
inhaling emptiness; my thoughts,
angeluses of the way's weather

become songs of imagination's heat.
My floating body now is husbanded
by the poems of my life,
my earthen self, white-ashed,
no more to be made wife.

The Mermaid

Compared with other women's loves,
none like you. As day, the night,
I must have you for quietude,
as the moon's peace, the sea.
Rising, her light gives off
fluorescence, like spilling fish.

These years, the rushes of silence.
Where shall I turn?
There is no road.
Only that empty page,
the seamless water & the path
through it, my words divide.

JAN KEMP

Elegy for a Schoolmate

On the other side of the world I heard
That she died in a Newton kitchen,
Her head in someone else's oven.

I'd never thumped her nor called her names
With the others, and so I had nothing
To sorrow or anger about.

Her big
Wet-nosed face just the same for me
As if she was sitting in the desk beside me.

Her clothes were always dirty
And she said stupid things.
The stupidest when she was trying hardest.

And I wish now that I'd thrown
A rock at her, had her caned for smoking . . .
Then I could feel pent-up for a day
And forget her.

But she takes her place among immortal things.
With the potter's wheel at the bottom of a dry pit,
With the hands of Egyptian ladies held like thin, brown leaves,
Their collars of beaten gold, and a basalt dog.

The Children

We are the children born
with tongues leafy as old lettuces.

Our green eyes are a fire
that had burned right down before we saw it,

our hands blue
like the Virgin's holy mantle

because we have held them up,
oh, ever so long,
against the sky.

Or brown, from pressing all night
against varnished doors.

When we walk along the road,
nothing ever happens.

The puddles stay as wet as ever,
dust falls from the pines onto our heads.
And the youngest of us say 'perfume, perfume!'
and will skip as the word pleases,
say '*bijoux*' and '*oiseaux*'
and in open daylight
jump at the sounds as though we were in a tunnel.

We are the children
who know the tricks of silence,
the cold minutes stacked to make an igloo.

Why do we think the sun
is a dirty coin?
why do we envy the yellow garters
on the skinny wasps?

Come inside, come inside,
it's late and we hadn't noticed.
Don't you know
the big white plates are watching for us?

VINCENT O'SULLIVAN

Clown, and all the sea behind him

He's very odd, standing on yellow sand.
His grey and crimson, satin, three-inch diamonds

agitate the smallest children most.
The older ones keep saying it's plain silly,

but they know, these others, it's more elaborate madness.
It's planned before like the concrete tower's planned

to hide the sun in the mornings. See him turning now
like the steps that go round the tower and round the sky.

The diamonds over his heart are stained, like tea
that's spilt on a patchwork quilt, and made it run.

He shouldn't have ever come to the beach like that.
He's got sand as well in his pom-poms,

that ugly stain, and his hat's lost somewhere, surely
Only spiky hair, a kind of dirty grass.

When you ask him to take a pigeon from under his arm
he lifts his arm and laughs when nothing happens.

'So, he's been drinking has he? a father says.
The girls are called to come back and his coloured diamonds

go shiny click this way, dark, dark, that,
until he moves so quickly, going round,

he's winding the afternoon sun like a wire on him,
he's a reel with yards and yards of sunset to him.

His costume's gone to his mind. Leave him alone.
A clown, and all the sea behind him.

He's a bird turning his cage to another bird.

VINCENT O'SULLIVAN

Contributors

Lawrence Bourke, Canberra, A.C.T.

Radharani Chakravarty, Delhi University.

Veena Noble Dass, Vanita Mahavidyalaya, Hyderabad.

R.K. Dhawan, Delhi University

Riemke Ensing, University of Auckland

Suzette Henke, University of Louisville, Kentucky

Jan Kemp, University of Singapore

Alison Lambert, Dutton Park, Queensland

Indibar Mukherjee, Patna University

Vincent O'Sullivan, renowned New Zealand poet

Som Prakash, Flinders University of South Australia

S. Ramaswamy, Bangalore University

David Ray, U.S.A

K.Venkata Reddy, S.K. University, Anantapur

Alan Riach, University of Waikato

Paul Sharrad, University of Wollongong

Valerie Sutherland, Brunswick, Victoria

Walter Tonetto, Melbourne

Marshall Walker, University of Waikato

Patrick L. West, University of Melbourne

INDEX